The Operas of Benjamin Britten
An Introduction

Also by Patricia Howard
Gluck and the Birth of Modern Opera

PATRICIA HOWARD

The Operas of
Benjamin
Britten
An Introduction

PRAEGER PUBLISHERS
NEW YORK · WASHINGTON

BOOKS THAT MATTER

Published in the United States of America in 1969
by Praeger Publishers, Inc.,
111 Fourth Avenue, New York, N.Y. 10003
Second printing 1970

© 1969, in London, England, by Patricia Howard

Library of Congress Catalog Card Number: 69-17084

PRINTED IN GREAT BRITAIN

For Lucy and Polly

Contents

Foreword

This book had its origin in some lectures given at the Dorking Institute of Further Education. My aim has been to expand these in two directions: to cover more operas and to reach a wider audience. Because I am writing for potential opera audiences rather than scholars I have not included a work which they are unlikely to have the opportunity of seeing—*Paul Bunyan*. I have also omitted Britten's edition of *The Beggar's Opera*, because I am concerned here only with composer/librettist operations, not with the different problems of arrangements and editions.

Acknowledgements

I would like to thank those who generously gave their permission to quote from works whose rights they control. These include:
Boosey and Hawkes Music Publishers Ltd. and Boosey and Hawkes Inc., for permission to quote from the scores of *Peter Grimes* (copyright 1945), *The Rape of Lucretia* (1946, 1947, 1949), *Albert Herring* (1948), *Little Sweep* (1949), *Billy Budd* (1951), *Gloriana* (1953), *The Turn of the Screw* (1955), *Noye's Fludde* (text from *English Miracle Plays, Moralities and Interludes*, edited by Alfred W. Pollard, by agreement with Clarendon Press, Oxford; copyright 1958), and *A Midsummer Night's Dream*; Faber Music Ltd., for the quotations from *Curlew River* and *The Burning Fiery Furnace*; and Mrs A. S. Strachey and Chatto and Windus for leave to quote from *Elizabeth and Essex*, by Lytton Strachey.

I also want to make the following personal acknowledgements: to Mrs Veronica Pritchard, Captain Peter Charig, R.N. (Retd.) and Mr William Plomer, for much factual help, and to my husband for constructively tampering with the manuscript at all stages of its development.

Chapter one

Peter Grimes

Libretto by Montagu Slater from the poem *The Borough* (1810) by George Crabbe. First performed at Sadler's Wells, June 1945.

CHARACTERS

PETER GRIMES, a fisherman — Peter Pears, *tenor*

ELLEN ORFORD, a widow, schoolmistress — Joan Cross, *soprano*

AUNTIE, landlady of "The Boar" — Edith Coates, *contralto*

1ST NIECE ⎱ main attractions of "The — Blanche Turner, *soprano*
2ND NIECE ⎰ Boar" — Minnia Bower, *soprano*

CAPTAIN BALSTRODE, retired merchant skipper — Roderick Jones, *baritone*

MRS SEDLEY, a rentier widow of an East India Company's factor — Valetta Jacopi, *mezzo-soprano*

SWALLOW, a lawyer — Owen Brannigan, *bass*

NED KEENE, apothecary and quack — Edmund Donlevy, *baritone*

ROBERT BOLES, fisherman and Methodist — Morgan Jones, *tenor*

REV. HORACE ADAMS, the rector — Tom Culbert, *tenor*

HOBSON, carrier — Frank Vaughan, *bass*

BOY, apprentice to Grimes — Leonard Thompson, *silent*

CHORUS of townspeople and fisherfolk

Conductor: Reginald Goodall
Producer: Eric Crozier
Scenery and Costumes: Kenneth Green
Chorus Master: Alan Melville

The story takes place in the Borough, a small fishing town on the East coast, towards 1830.

PROLOGUE: The Moot Hall at the inquest on the death of Peter Grimes's apprentice. The evidence is inconclusive and Swallow, the coroner, advises Grimes: "Do not get another boy apprentice. Get a fisherman to help you, big enough to stand up for himself." Grimes is bitter about the verdict, "died in accidental circumstances", which gives plenty of scope to the gossips. When the court is cleared, Ellen Orford, the schoolmistress, offers her sympathy and plans a new start for Grimes.

ACT I, SCENE I: A street by the sea, a few days later. Ned Keene, the apothecary, has found a new apprentice for Grimes. Since the inquest Grimes has been shunned by most of the Borough, but he is not entirely friendless—Balstrode, a retired merchant skipper, and Keene help him to haul his boat, and Ellen Orford goes with Carter Hobson to fetch the apprentice. Balstrode announces the coming storm and when everyone has retired to their own homes or "The Boar" he finds Grimes still working at his boat. Balstrode, like Swallow and Ellen, suggests a new beginning for Grimes, but Grimes is not willing to take his advice and reveals his plan to marry Ellen, even if he has to "fish the sea dry" to offer her respectability.

SCENE 2: "The Boar" the same night. The storm is raging outside. Within, everyone is on edge; the situation is not improved by the hysterical Mrs Sedley awaiting her supply of laudanum, drunken Bob Boles, the Methodist preacher, and

Grimes's wild entry and poetic utterance which provokes "He's mad or drunk" from the crowd. At last Ellen arrives with the boy, whom Grimes insists on immediately taking away to his lonely hut.

ACT II, SCENE I: Sunday morning, a few weeks later. Ellen and the new apprentice are on the beach while Matins is in progress in the parish church. Ellen discovers that the boy's clothes are torn and he is bruised—"well, it's begun", she says. Grimes enters, to take the boy fishing and when Ellen argues that it is his holiday Grimes replies, "This is whatever day I say it is!" They quarrel, Grimes strikes Ellen and roughly takes the boy with him. The news that "Grimes is at his exercise" soon runs through the Borough and, roused to ferocity, the men form a party to investigate Grimes at his hut.

SCENE 2: Meanwhile Grimes is preparing to go fishing. Just as he is about to set out he hears the procession approaching his hut. The boy starts out down the cliff and falls to his death. Grimes hurries after him and the party arrives to find a "neat and empty hut".

ACT III, SCENE I: The beach and street a few nights later. A dance is taking place in the Moot Hall. Everyone appears to have forgotten Grimes for the moment, except Mrs Sedley, who overhears Balstrode tell Ellen that Grimes's boat is in— and that the boy's jersey has been washed in by the tide. Mrs Sedley rouses Swallow and Hobson to form a search party to find Grimes.

SCENE 2: A few hours later. A thick fog is everywhere; the fog-horn and the cries of the searchers can be heard distantly. Peter Grimes is exhausted and almost insane. When Ellen and Balstrode discover him by his boat. Balstrode tells him to take his boat out and sink it: which he does. With the dawn life begins again in the Borough.

With hindsight we can see *Peter Grimes* to be in many ways typical of Britten's operatic subjects. The East Anglian background runs through four of the first ten operas. The portrayal of the individual in conflict with society is a more important theme. The detailed portrait of an enclosed community, whether a nation or the inmates of an isolated country house, is a part of all the operas. The musical treatment is also at one with the succeeding works. Opera is a blunt instrument; compared with the conversation of chamber music it is public speech: it addresses itself to an audience—in Britten's later operas it tends to do this explicitly in the Prologues.

Already in *Peter Grimes*, however, Britten's method at times tends towards the chamber-music approach that later became an inevitable development, artistically as well as economically. Grimes does no public speaking. In an intimacy of style unparalleled, I find, since Handel, Grimes's character reveals itself in a dramatically restrained and almost wholly musical dimension. All that he *does* in the opera is to strike Ellen and mildly manhandle the boy. The rest is style. The most dramatic events in the opera—the death of the boy and the death of Grimes—are ignored musically. This is not what the opera is about.

The Prologue, for example—the inquest on the death of Grimes's previous apprentice—is not so much concerned with putting across the incidents which led up to the death (Grimes covers these far more fluently in his conversation with Balstrode in Act I, Scene 1) as with making concrete and visual Grimes's psychological predicament: not only one man against a crowd, but one man put on trial, informally, illegally, by the crowd. Structurally the scene is a through-composed movement with a coda for Grimes and Ellen.

(Ellen is tentatively aligned with Grimes in the trial, not too closely, because he has to be seen in dramatic isolation; but her loyalty is firmly expressed in the coda-duet, at first mitigated by the "cross-purposes" of bitonality, then deludedly united with Grimes in unison.)

Vocally, the Prologue establishes the characters of Swallow, Grimes, Ellen, and to a large extent the Borough. Visually, we also get individual impressions of the Rector, Boles, Auntie, and Mrs Sedley. The backbone of the instrumental music is the busy, important-sounding opening four bars— soon associated with the self-important Swallow. We see him as a rigidly efficient lawyer, yet unscrupulously "feeding" the gossips:

EX. I.

Grimes is very much changed from the villain of Crabbe's poem. The tragedy of his situation lies in the paradox that while he is whole-heartedly of the Borough, "rooted here", he does not speak the same language. The tragedy of his character cannot be expressed so concisely. An anti-villain, he behaves neither villainously nor nobly; in compensation for his inability to deal with life, he has highly articulate "waking dreams", but the aspirations he expresses in his dreams are translated only in material terms in every-day life. Grimes cannot make any specific moves towards marrying Ellen, because this marriage, and the idyllic home, are part of his dream life. We can see early on in the opera

that the marriage is bound to remain a dream, since Grimes's
only approach to it is over materialistic hurdles of profits and
"golden opinions"—and these Grimes is manifestly incapable
of winning. Much of this is conveyed in the first notes he sings,
or rather in the chord change in the orchestra:

EX. 2.

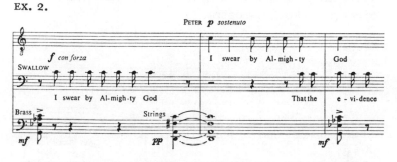

Six orchestral interludes introduce the six scenes of the
opera. Roughly generalising, we can describe the act Intro-
ductions, I, III, and V as expository, and the inter-scene
Interludes, II, IV, and VI as developmental. From another
point of view, the first group are primarily tone pictures of
the sea—almost a character in the drama; and the second
group analytical of Grimes's character. (Interlude II somewhat disturbs the neatness of this, since it is undoubtedly
portraying the physical storm, and only towards the end are
we explicitly shown that it is the turbulence of Grimes's
character that is at issue.)

Act I, Scene 1: the Borough at work. There are two types of
choruses in *Peter Grimes*: we have already heard, in the court-
room scene, a cluster of small choruses of the first type—the
Borough "at its exercise", gossiping, looking outwards at
Grimes. The music is imitative of conversational tones. (It is
also usually imitative!) In the court-room scene, in fact, it is
only the style of the music that puts the choruses in this category—the words are formalised aphorisms that fall short of
the spontaneous effect of the music. "Look out for squalls" in

this scene and "Talk of the devil" in the next are more typical. The second type of chorus is the choral movement, a vocal equivalent of the interludes, with the Borough looking inwards at itself—but not too closely—and drawing, in the ceremony of regular phrases and architectural melodic lines, a deceptively innocuous portrait. It is a chorus of this sort that opens (and closes) the opera:

EX. 3.

(The first interlude continues in the orchestra and underlies much of the subsequent scene.)

It is a long choral movement, loosely enclosing brief scenes of recitative in which the minor characters of the Borough are delineated briefly and memorably. The libretto does not give the music the chance to be at all subtle in the recitative and informal ensembles; it is very mannered—nearly as much so as in *Lucretia* without the justification of a consciously artificial style, an attribute of the later opera—and flows in statements and observations rather than communications. And so we are never tricked—as I think we are in *Billy Budd* and *The Turn of the Screw*—into thinking that this is how the characters normally express themselves:

> Had Auntie no nieces we'd never respect her
> You jeer, but if they wink you're eager to follow
> A man should have hobbies to cheer his private life

This results, at any rate, in keeping the minor characters minor; there is a kaleidoscopic effect as they emerge from and rejoin the corporate character of the Borough—or hover on the edge as Balstrode does when the first man-hunt begins— which occurs again in *Billy Budd* and gives detail and realism to potentially slow-moving and formal choral scenes.

The continuous movement stops when Grimes appears. Who will help him haul his boat? This instantly divides— very unequally—the bystanders. In a short ensemble Balstrode and Keene range themselves on Grimes' side by helping him. They sing a capstan song, above which Auntie expresses her disinterest in the Grimes-baiting situation and Boles, the Methodist preacher, denounces Grimes. The short self-contained forms are linked by continuing references to the material of the first interlude; it underlies a conversational passage in which Ned Keene reveals that he has obtained a new apprentice for Grimes. Another formal scheme begins with the miniature air of Hobson the carter, "I have to go from pub to pub"—a further example of the individualisation, albeit stylised, of a member of the Borough. Chorus interjections, of the "gossip" type, are incorporated in the aria. Ellen, who aligns herself with Grimes in the unison cadence of the Prologue, now links herself with the carter. She repeats his short air to the words:

> The boy needs comfort late at night,
> He needs a welcome on the road,

Coming here strange he'll be afraid—
I'll mind your passenger!

Elements of this tune become the bass of the next brief gossip
chorus, "Ellen, you're leading us a dance", and a free conversion of two ideas in it becomes the basis of Ellen's first
important aria:

EX. 4

Andante con moto : largamente

The heavy triplets of Hobson's "picking up parcels" are
opened out into this irregular, liquid rhythm. The descending
scale is not only an inversion of "my journey back is late at
night" but also a shape which is going to become characteristic of Ellen's music. It is this scale that is extended upwards
in the ensuing dialogue between the grotesque Mrs Sedley,
and Ned Keene. Mrs Sedley, "a rentier widow of an East
India Company's factor", comes far nearer to being the
villain of the opera than Grimes, nearer even than the corporate character of the Borough, which is redeemed by its
mixed motives. Yet this deeply serious tragedy is continually
prodded along, poked into action and finally driven to inevitability by the machinations of this comic caricature.

The scene finale begins. The pattern for this extended ensemble is used repeatedly in the opera. It combines the two
types of chorus previously described. To begin, the named
characters have a *largamente* commentary on the action:

EX. 5

(The intervals of these first four notes are to permeate the rest of the scene, the following interlude, and intermittently the second scene of the act.) Against this the Chorus have an action or gossip-style chorus, "Look out for squalls, It's veering in from sea, Look the storm cone, The wind veers in at gale force." The pattern is reversed when the Chorus have the *largamente* phrase and the soloists continue with their quick-moving counter-subject. The diverse forces are drawn together dramatically for the phrase:

EX. 6

O   tide—   that waits for no man,   spare   our   coasts!

This unanimous, spontaneous utterance by the Chorus and lesser principals is paralleled in the last act of the opera, the "Peter Grimes" halloos of the man-hunt. The opera makes great use of verbal and melodic quotations and retrospections towards its end; this is an instance in which it also quotes a sonority.

The end of the scene is a great contrast: in a dialogue, Balstrode tries to make closer contact with Grimes. They both recall the Prologue—Grimes in the *sostenuto* phrase on one note, "I live alone, the habit grows", and Balstrode, quoting Swallow's music, "Then the crowner sits to hint but not to mention crimes/And publishes an open verdict whispered about this Peter Grimes." Grimes also recalls the storm in which his first apprentice died; the semitone motif of the actual incipient storm is rephrased as a minor ninth. Major and minor, this is an important interval in his music, epitomising his larger than life-size stature in the drama as well as the perpetual longing for the unattainable with which he is

tormented. In contrast, we see him as the utterly ineffectual
man of action in "They listen to money". Rhythmically, he is
literally attempting to beat the Borough of the gossip-choruses
at its own game. Finally we have the, as it were, *da capo* of
this portrait of Grimes. Left alone he sings:

EX. 7

The storm-derived minor ninth expands into the major: the
unattainable vision he gropes after.

This scene is an exposition. More than the Prologue, it is
an introduction to the Borough—its way of life, its trades,
its vital dependence on unpropitious elements. With virtuosity it depicts a society of individuals which is nevertheless
a community. Grimes is an everpresent factor in the scene.
Spontaneous judgements, for and against him, are made on
every side. Balstrode, in the storm-ensemble, appears as a
kind of leader—not too influential, though: he converts no
one by helping Grimes. (He comes nearest in this opera to
being a character with whom the audience can identify, but
is not drawn quite fully enough to sustain this role.)

The second scene of the act is tenser because it is less expansive in scope. It is physically claustrophobic because the
community (or sufficient representatives of it) is confined
within "The Boar"; emotionally, because of the storm which
has raged throughout the orchestral interlude II, and—
superb dramatic device—bursts in upon the inmates of "The
Boar" whenever anyone opens and struggles to shut the door.
This and the imminent arrival of Grimes's new apprentice
keep everyone on edge, and the individual incidents with
Mrs Sedley and the drunken Boles intensify rather than relieve
the mood.

The storm interlude is based on the first four notes of Ex. 5, extended in a semitonal "worrying" pattern derived from Balstrode's line in his dialogue with Grimes at the end of Scene 1. It is developed into the large-scale evocation of the storm which is necessary to prepare for the atmosphere sustained in the following scene. We have to remember that it is there even when "The Boar's" door is shut. Towards the end of the interlude the *da capo* section of Grimes's aria is referred to: it is not, I think, making a big dramatic point here. The storm is too patently physical for us to associate it with Grimes's maladjustments. It is drawing a simile, not a metaphor; a comparison, not an identification.

In the conversation of various minor characters that opens the second scene we can discern how much easier it is to establish caricature figures—the nieces and Auntie—than the somewhat more weighty ones—Balstrode and Keene—particularly in the absence of Grimes. It is their relationship with him, the simple fact that it is unprejudiced, that is their dramatic justification and it is also on this point that their characterisation depends. When Grimes is not about, their importance and their effectiveness are reduced. Balstrode does, however, lead another ensemble of the inward-looking type—"We live and let live and look/We keep our hands to ourselves." This has a horrifying irony which cannot be fully appreciated at this point in the opera.

When Grimes enters it is not the actual storm that bursts through the door with him but the storm he carries about within him: the scale passage figures initially belonged to the storm after which his first apprentice died; the bass mutters of "terrors and tragedies" that he aspired to banish in the *da capo* section of that monologue, the big interval is the minor ninth, not the major—an ominous entrance! This entrance becomes continuous with Grimes's second aria, "Now the Great Bear and Pleiades"—the interpolated conversation and whispered gossip chorus ("Talk of the devil and there he is") hang fire over an E pedal—this makes it seem a continuous statement, a strong stroke of characterisation. There is little enough to take hold of in Grimes's character.

His aria is a beautifully constructed piece. It is strophic— the words strictly and the music more freely. The voice sings repeated notes over a canonic exposition in the strings which is pulled up to a stationary chord when, in a cadenza-like flowering, the voice makes the fifth entry of the canon:

EX. 8

The last verse is split into an agitated passage, "But if the
horoscope's bewildering . . ." and a return to the mood of
the first verse—not exact, however, as there are only half as
many lines left, so the canon is compressed, this time working
down the instruments: "Who can turn skies back and begin
again?"

The importance of this number cannot be overestimated.
This is what the opera is about. Grimes—the new Grimes
created by Slater and Britten as opposed to Crabbe's villain
—is a most apt protagonist for an opera, in that his character
can only be fully revealed in music. I will go further and say
that it is only the complete beauty of this aria that makes the
drama a tragedy:

> To wicked spirits are horrid shapes assign'd,
> This beauteous form assures a piteous mind.

Here, certainly, we have a "beauteous" sound which assures
us of the essential good of the verbally uncommunicable
character of Peter Grimes.

The crowd in "The Boar" are, naturally, utterly be-
wildered. The pedal note that led up to the aria now becomes an inverted pedal over the confused chorus, not moving
off till Boles's taunt, "his exercise is not with men but killing
boys!" This is the first outspoken condemnation of Grimes—
following closely on the revelation of a musical character
which is certainly not that of a murderer—and it also introduces the curiously sinister expression "exercise" which is to
be important in the next act.

They sing a round to keep the peace. It is a dramatic
incident which, like the Prologue, demonstrates the larger
situation: the community conforms, Grimes cannot (his entry
in augmentation recalls the Prologue—as in his characterising
interval of the ninth he is again larger than life) and he is
finally overwhelmed and obliterated by the conformists. The
denouement of the drama is here, in musical terms, though

we can only see this when we know what is going to happen.

After this, an abrupt close—Ellen, Hobson, and the apprentice arrive, and the storm music takes over in the orchestra till the end of the scene. One point worth mentioning is that Ellen sings the phrase "Peter will take you home" (to the apprentice) to notes which outline, with one intermediate step, Grimes's major ninth—his idyllic home, and Ellen's, too, after she has identified herself with Grimes in the closing duet of the Prologue. The crowd take up her notes; they do not actually sing Grimes's ninth, but jump the major sixth from the intermediate step ("Home! Do you call that home!"), ending, however, with the fall from F to E♭ which represents the accomplishment of his aspirations. It is a kind of profanation. There are no specifically religious issues in *Peter Grimes*. The situation, the action and the motivation of the characters could hardly be more wordly. Even Grimes cannot see a way to attain a spiritual life without vanquishing the world on its own terms. Nevertheless the *music* of Grimes's arias is so numinously aware that attempts to break in upon it by the uninitiated become a blasphemy which direct our sympathies firmly towards Grimes, even at this moment when he is obviously oblivious to the boy's needs.

In the second act, the interlude again continues into the first scene. It is a Sunday morning. The sunlight, the waves, and the music all glitter with innocence in this tension-free setting. Ellen now becomes the voice of the new apprentice —we have already seen her identify herself with Grimes and Hobson—"Shall I tell you what your life was like?" She is portrayed not only as one who sides with Grimes—that would be too limited a portrait of her, besides weakening Grimes's isolation—but as one who in general is capable of sympathy: the enlightened, educated member of the Borough (in conspicuous contrast to the Rector).

It is another two-layer scene, like the storm and the "Boar"

interior. The organ and congregation can be heard intermittently against the dialogue or, rather, monologue, as the boy
never speaks. It is another aspect of the very complete portrayal of the community: we are never allowed to forget
their presence. Of course, it provides a useful opportunity
for dramatic comment and irony:

> ELLEN: John, you may have heard the story of the
>   prentice Peter had before.
> CONGREGATION: . . . and shades of night return once
>   more.
> ELLEN: John, what are you trying to hide?
> CONGREGATION: O Lord, open Thou our lips.

The irrelevance of the congregation's words to the situation
on the beach is as revealing as their unconscious aptness—
when Ellen discovers the bruise, and the continuation of the
horror that this implies, the congregation bursts in with a
fortissimo "Gloria". Ellen's aria ,"Child you're not too young
to know where roots of sorrow are", obliterates the church
music with its intensity.

The changing numbers of the liturgy follow the changing
dramatic situation. The congregation begin the *"Benedicite"*.
Its expression of undiscriminating energy accompanies
Grimes's entrance—he has seen a shoal and wants to take the
apprentice off fishing at once. Ellen remonstrates that this is
the boy's agreed day of rest. Grimes's reply is sinister: "He
works for me, leave him alone, he's mine!" Ellen has a dark,
expressive phrase, taken from the setting of the Benedicite—
"This unrelenting work, this grey unresting industry, What
aim, what future, what peace will your hard profits buy?"
Grimes answers with "Buy us a home, buy us respect"—a
continuation of "They listen to money" in Act I, Scene 1.

To the notes of the derisive "Do you call that home!" from
the previous scene (Ellen briefly identified as a prying out-
sider), she sings: "Peter, tell me one thing, where the

youngster got that ugly bruise?" completing the phrase in
her scale-wise melodic idiom. Grimes answers only in minor
ninths, but he is later moved by Ellen to adopt her style for
the phrase "My only hope depends on you, if you take it away
what's left?"—that this is a forlorn hope we can at this stage
guess, because Grimes has no language within his own style
to convey this tenderness. He soon reverts to his own idiom:

EX. 9

Ellen expresses what Grimes cannot face: "We were mistaken
to have dreamed—Peter! We've failed." In his despair he
strikes her; from the church (which has been silent for some
time) comes an Amen and Grimes breaks out with:

EX. 10

This scene reveals all that up to now has been mere rumour
and suspicion to be fact—the boy has a bruise, Grimes strikes
Ellen. We witness this unwillingly. To give our revulsion
outlets other than Grimes, there follows another view of the
Borough "at its exercise".

Ex. 10 sets in motion an extended number involving much
musical and dramatic interest. It is enunciated in a backwards
version of the "Great Bear" scheme: Grimes's phrase sets the
orchestra (this time the brass) off in canon. The phrase itself
expresses the utter inevitability of the whole tragedy. As in
the storm chorus in Act I, Britten combines naturalistic
chorus material—the sort I have been calling gossip-style—
"What is it? What do you suppose?"—with (in the full

meaning of the word) the artificial phrase of Ex. 10—"Grimes
is at his exercise!" (A strange, vivid, pregnant expression that
whips the Borough, with the exception of Balstrode and Ellen,
into a mood of general accusation.) The pace increases. The
attention of the Borough focuses on Ellen. A brassy theme
like a revivalist hymn is shared by Boles and the Chorus,
contrasted with another fine *semplice* melody for Ellen: "We
planned that their lives should have a new start." Auntie and
Balstrode side with Ellen, but the others turn on her with
increasing venom. The accompaniment speed and dynamic
level increase again (*"strepitoso, archi-strepitoso e strepitosissimo!"*)
and the wealth of ill feeling is formalised by the Rector and
Swallow as they assemble the vigilante procession. Hobson's
drum stresses the primitive nature of the ceremony:

> Now is gossip put on trial,
> Now the rumours either fail,
> Or are shouted in the wind,
> Sweeping furious through the land . . .
> Now the whispers stand out,
> Now confronted by the fact,
> Bring the branding iron and knife,
> What's done now is done for life.

The men of the Borough set off on their witch (warlock?)
hunt. The women remain, and sing unsatisfactory words to
enchanting music.

The fourth interlude is a set of nine variations on an eloquent viola theme—a decorated descending fifth—over a
passacaglia bass derived from Ex. 10. It is unutterably sad.
Once more it continues into the scene where it is shown to be
concerned with Grimes, particularly in his relationship with
the apprentices. Fragments of the variations return between
his shouted comments to the boy—he is in a "towering rage"
with himself for his quarrel with Ellen and he turns this upon
the boy. Again he develops the "they listen to money" argu-

ment. The fulfilment of his mercenary ambition sounded improbable in Act I—here it appears as self-deluding as the vision of the "kindlier home" he dwells on next. When Grimes sings of this imaginary life with Ellen, as in the last scene his melodic line takes on the shape of hers ("And she would soon forget her schoolhouse ways . . ."). Like all Grimes's vision arias, it is a feast of sensuous beauty.

We hear the Borough procession before Grimes does—he is still listening to "those voices that will not be drowned". They approach gradually. Grimes dispatches the boy down the cliff edge as they knock at the door. We clearly see that Grimes is nowhere near his apprentice when he falls; but his demonstrable innocence comes too late. No one will believe any good of him now. The search party enter the hut and find it empty. Like their attempted entry into Grimes's musical "home" in the scene in "The Boar", this physical entry has a feeling of violation. They make a comic anti-climax after the fury of emotion that prompted their procession, and the intensity of musical experience in the hut scene. In fact, they are little more than a brief interruption. When they leave, Balstrode is left alone in the hut to examine the boy's discarded clothes and to climb down the cliff after Grimes. What we hear is, in fact, the tenth variation of the passacaglia: the music returns to the viola theme of the interlude (inverted), accompanied by the celesta figuration which appeared when the boy fell. There is one final statement of the passacaglia bass.

The third act opens with the last "sea interlude"; an uncomplicated evocation of the sea at night. The scene is the village street, a dance is taking place in the Moot Hall, "The Boar" is doing a flourishing trade—again we see the Borough community about their habitual occupations and recreations. Musically it is a two-tiered scene once more, with a dance band off-stage which plays a substantial part in accompanying the dialogue. New light is still being cast on the minor characters: Swallow (as a ludicrous lover), the Rector, and above all Mrs Sedley, whose malice goes far beyond the capacity for idle rumour of the other Borough inhabitants:

Crime that my hobby is by cities hoarded.
Rarely are country minds lifted to murder,
The noblest of my crimes which are my study.
And now the crime is here and I am ready!

She overhears Balstrode—in a dialogue punctuated by references to the passacaglia bass (for the first time the dance band has a prolonged silence)—telling Ellen that Grimes's boat is back (he has been missing for some days), and that he, Balstrode, has found the boy's jersey washed in by the tide. This prompts Ellen to sing the most concentrated and deeply tragic aria in her part, "Embroidery in childhood was a luxury of idleness". Like all the lyrical music in the opera, its form is transparently clear. All the resources of organisation are in the melodic line. This is thrown into bold relief as it is surrounded by recitative on a monotone. Ellen and Balstrode pledge their loyalty to Grimes in a canonic development of the Ex. 10 phrase, a further identification of Ellen, and now of Balstrode, too, with Grimes. The Borough is shown to be antagonistic towards Grimes when they do not hold any evidence against him, while Ellen and Balstrode, knowing some and suspecting more of the tragedy, choose this moment to align themselves with him.

Mrs Sedley manages to alert Swallow and Hobson to set up a new search for Grimes. Her creeping chromatic music accompanies a new gossip chorus—"Who holds himself apart lets his pride rise,/Him who despises us we'll destroy" (uncomfortable words again, to represent spontaneous speech). The chromatic theme is developed into a wider-ranging line as the minor principals join the Chorus to create another big ensemble in the style of the storm chorus and "Grimes is at his exercise"—the Chorus and soloists merge and re-emerge

in the ensemble just as their characters are at times individualised and at times identified with the Borough. Subsequently
a Ländler tune which was previously played by the dance
band becomes a wordless climax to this second man-hunt—
distinguished from the Act II procession by the absence of
even a pretence at law and order. Hobson's drum was spine-
chilling in the second act, but it was controlled and purposeful; here, the use of the dance tune implies the irresponsibility
of the singers, their wordless fury suggests hysteria. Then the
cries of "Peter Grimes" build up, through the ensemble. The
scene ends with concerted halloos recalling earlier impassioned outbursts by the crowd: "O tide that waits for no
man . . ." and "Home? Do you call that home!"

Interlude, VI, like IV, is wholly a Grimes interlude. It
shows in musical terms his mental breakdown. The form this
takes is predictable. Grimes throughout the opera has shown
a tendency to repeat himself (in itself a characteristic of a
lonely man) and to dwell repeatedly on his worldly ambi-
tions—"they listen to money" has already occurred three
times. He has been shown to dress his Ellen-orientated dreams
in Ellen's vocal style (at least twice), to associate his sense of
an undeserved evil fate with the motif in which he first
realised this. (Ex. 10, and its inversion when he blames the
apprentice in the hut scene for being "the cause of everything". It is, of course, not the apprentice's fault. It is Grimes's
—for being himself—and this point the music conveys to the
audience if not to Grimes). This interlude contains fragments
of all these, linked by a sustained D F♯ C chord on the horns.
When the scene begins, the off-stage Chorus take over the
horn chord for their distant cry of "Grimes". A (tuba) fog-
horn adds an E♭ phrasing-off to D; the fog represents dramatically both the physical and mental confusion of the scene,
as in the second act of *Billy Budd*. This semitone which appears
on the fog-horn—really Grimes's minor ninth deprived of the
energy to overshoot the octave—dominates the fragmentary

vocal line when Grimes enters, "weary and demented", recalling vocally, as the interlude did instrumentally, earlier
scenes in the opera. The recollections are always distorted:
the music in which Swallow at the inquest offered a new start
to Grimes ("Peter Grimes I here advise you . . .") is sung
to words which helped to hound him ("accidental circumstances"); the notes to which he earlier sang "I'll marry
Ellen" and resolved to "get money to choke down rumour's
throat" here contain the failure of his plans: "the argument's
finished, friendship lost, gossip is shouting". The off-stage
shouts of "Peter Grimes" approach and recede in the fog.
When they are very loud and near, Grimes "roars back at the
shouters" his own name. This is perhaps the most horrifying
moment in the scene. Ellen and Balstrode find him, but he
is no longer aware of Ellen. He sings the major ninth dream-
consummation music, "what harbour shelters peace" (Ex. 7).
In spoken words, Balstrode tells him to "sail out until you
lose sight of the Moot Hall. Then sink the boat. . . ." There
is no musical portrayal of his death because it has been (as in
Lucretia) anticipated in the preceding minutes.

The music reverts to the first interlude and the opening
chorus—slowly at first, speeding up with the dawn. "Rumour"
of a boat sinking out at sea is dismissed *as* a rumour: the
final irony. I think we hate the Chorus in this closing scene.
It is an opera so full of judgements, right and wrong, misguided and wilfully malicious, that the audience is compelled
to react very strongly to it. Its miracle is that a character as
unattractive, unapproachable, and undeniably unpleasant as
Grimes in the end manages to gain our sympathy. His is not
a character with whom we can admit to identifying ourselves;
yet his musical character is one to which we listen not with
pity, but with delight.

B

Chapter two

The Rape of Lucretia

Libretto by Ronald Duncan from a play *Le Viol de Lucrèce* (1931), by André Obey.
First performed at Glyndebourne, July 1946.

CHARACTERS

MALE CHORUS	{ Peter Pears, *tenor* Aksel Schiotz
FEMALE CHORUS	{ Joan Cross, *soprano* Flora Nielsen
COLLATINUS, a Roman General	{ Owen Brannigan, *bass* Norman Walker
JUNIUS, a Roman General	{ Edmund Donlevy, *baritone* Frederick Sharp
TARQUINIUS, son of Tarquinius Super-bus, the Etruscan ruler of Rome	{ Otakar Kraus, *baritone* Frank Rogier
LUCRETIA, wife of Collatinus	{ Kathleen Ferrier, *contralto* Nancy Evans
BIANCA, Lucretia's old nurse	{ Anna Pollock, *mezzo-soprano* Catherine Lawson
LUCIA, a maid	{ Margaret Ritchie, *soprano* Lesley Duff

Conductors: Ernest Ansermet and Reginald Goodall
Producer: Eric Crozier
Designer: John Piper
Director of Musical Studies: Hans Oppenheim

ACT I, INTRODUCTION: The Male and Female Choruses paint the background to the rise of the Tarquins and the Graeco-Roman war. They reveal that they will witness the tragedy of Lucretia and Tarquinius "through eyes which once have wept with Christ's own tears".

SCENE I: The General's tent in the camp ouside Rome. Tarquinius, Junius, and Collatinus, three Roman generals, are drinking together, discussing the wager which took place the previous night which proved Lucretia to be the only virtuous wife. Junius tempts Tarquinius to "prove Lucretia chaste". Tarquinius calls for his horse and rides to Rome.

SCENE 2: A room in Lucretia's house in Rome, the same evening. Lucretia is at home with her women, Bianca and Lucia; Tarquinius arrives and requires hospitality for the night.

ACT II, INTRODUCTION: The Male and Female Choruses again fill in the political history of the Etruscan domination of Rome.

SCENE I: Lucretia's bedroom. Lucretia is asleep. Tarquinius wakes her, overcomes her resistance, and ravishes her. The Choruses sing a hymn to the Virgin.

SCENE 2: A room in Lucretia's house, the next morning. Bianca and Lucia are arranging flowers in the bright sunlight. Lucretia enters, subdued, with barely controlled hysteria which breaks out when she is given the doubly symbolic orchids to arrange. She sends a message for Collatinus to come to her and in her distraction weaves the flowers into a wreath. Collatinus arrives with Junius. Lucretia enters, in mourning; she tells Collatinus what has happened, rejects his forgiveness and consolation and stabs herself. The assembled characters lament her death and the transience of life. The Male and Female Choruses, from their Christian standpoint, offer a vision of redemption and eternal life.

Schütz, after the economic depredations of the Thirty Years War, was required to abandon the resources he had previously called upon to perform his music, and wrote instead, in an austere and economical style, music for the austere and economical times in which he found himself. Opera in England has never been a financially flourishing concern (cause or effect of the sparse indigenous tradition?) and Britten's chamber operas are in part a result of this condition. However, opera aligned with the refinement of language of chamber music was predictably attractive to Britten, as was the opportunity for displaying individual vocal and instrumental personality and virtuosity. This opera must have been to some extent a conjunction of the congenial and the convenient. The play, too, seems apt for this treatment. André Obey's *Le Viol de Lucrèce* has in its two Narrators, who comment on and at times describe the action, an extra layer of theatrical manner that is useful in transforming a story into an opera. And chamber opera can employ the extra formality of some sort of framing device with advantage. *Albert Herring* has its expository first scene, *The Turn of the Screw*, a prologue, and the parables *Curlew River* and *The Burning Fiery Furnace* have the most elaborate framing of all, in the processions involving not only the singers but the orchestra, too—the participation in the visual drama of the instrumentalists is a development of the exposition of their personalities in the earlier chamber operas, *Lucretia* in particular.

The instruments chosen for *Lucretia* are comprehensive in their representation, apart from the absence of the brighter brass: flute (doubling piccolo and alto flute), oboe (doubling cor anglais), clarinet (doubling bass clarinet), bassoon, horn, percussion, harp, string quartet with double bass. The conductor plays the piano in the recitatives. The personality of each of these instruments is fully explored in the course of the opera.

There is no overture—no instrumental overture. There is instead an introduction by the Male and Female Choruses (Obey's narrators transformed into a pair of Christian commentators of didactic if not pedagogic inclinations) who, when the curtain rises, are discovered seated on either side of the stage reading from books of Roman history. This is a passage of recitative built around recurrent instrumental chord groups. The Male and Female Choruses have the most formal, unconversational recitative in the opera, but it is already a much more flexible language than in *Peter Grimes*—less reminiscent of the chordal and cadential shapes of eighteenth-century recitative, more closely derived from the words set and flowing more freely into passages of arioso:

EX. II

There is a hint of the exciting variety of sounds that can be produced with the chamber ensemble in the fragment of a march at the words "so here the grumbling Romans march from Rome . . .": double bass *col legno* and timpani in thirds, far below a high bassoon and soprano line. The introduction ends with the Male and Female Choruses' hymn— this is to recur—which explains their purpose as Christian interpreters of the action and also—they sing the same tune in octaves—unites the two motifs which are associated in general with Male and Female, and in particular with Tarquinius and Lucretia throughout the opera. As a first-time audience cannot at this stage know that they are motifs much less to whom or what they are attached, all that is conveyed by the hymn is a certain solemnity and formality; it is significant music, the significance of which has not yet been revealed.

The first scene is the camp outside Rome. After the recitative style of the introduction and the spare ceremonial of the hymn, the music now assumes a more expansive style, depicting the "thirsty evening" with muted strings and the harp representing "the noise of crickets" in a little five-note phrase that dominates the melodic line of the Male Chorus. The Male Chorus describes the mood, making explicit the function of the atmospheric music—there is not much independent instrumental music in *Lucretia*; it is from this point of view the most unambiguous of the operas as the choruses are always present verbally to define the drama when the protagonists of the opera are not singing.

The physical atmosphere is an incipient thunderstorm. The dramatic atmosphere is also pregnant with the quarrel that is to occur. Collatinus, Junius, and Tarquinius are discovered drinking and they sing a drinking song which is essentially competitive: their rivalry is never far below the surface, even in moments of apparent relaxation. In recitative the generals discuss the wager which took place the previous night, proving

Lucretia to be the only virtuous wife. This immediately divides the generals: Junius, bitter at his wife's unfaithfulness and suspicious of the political advantage Lucretia's chastity gives Collatinus; Tarquinius, detached and teasing except at the phrase:

EX. 12

This has a (literally) imperious ring, a conspicuous phrase, and important as being the first unconcealed appearance of the Tarquinius motif. Collatinus attempts the role of peacemaker and prompted by him, Tarquinius unites the trio in a toast:

EX. 13

a passage which certainly drives home the Lucretia motif in a sonorous well of sound, striking after the rapid quarrel dialogue.

In the second half of this scene—my division, not specifically Britten's or Duncan's—we see the men revealing themselves in more continuously lyrical and introspective music. (It is an intensely lyrical opera: the absence of a chorus in the conventional sense contributes to this. There is no music —not even the Ride to Rome—which makes a rhythmic impact at the expense of line. The motifs, on which the music is increasingly dependent, are linear in conception and application.) After the toast, Junius breaks out in a soliloquy aria of hate and jealousy. The Lucretia motif is tossed about in the voice part and woodwind: Junius is "sick of that name". There are not more than a couple of consecutive bars that do not carry some statement or fragment of it. The aria is musically (though not dramatically) a dialogue between Junius and the Male Chorus. The Male Chorus's coda contains a memorable melodic phrase:

EX. 14

which recurs three more times in the course of the opera. Against it we hear a typical transformation of the Lucretia motif into an accompanying figure for the harp.

The conversation that follows, between Collatinus and Junius, develops the implications of the Tarquinius motif, which also stands for all the male characters, just as Lucretia (and her motif) at times represents all women. The interval of a fourth is loosely associated with all the men; the diminished interval is usually linked with Tarquinius, the perfect with Collatinus. Here Collatinus sings almost wholly in descending and perfect fourths and Junius in ascending and perfect fourths against a string accompaniment of interlocking thirds (Lucretia). Collatinus's characteristically philosophically ponderous aria follows, interrupted by Tarquinius, who is still singing the drinking song from the beginning of the scene. Tarquinius is presented as an almost innocent character in this scene and indeed throughout the opera—an ignoble savage—compared with Collatinus he is attractively spontaneous and instinctive, compared with Junius he is a harmless enough friend. All the vice, in this dialogue, is on Junius's side:

TARQUINIUS: There goes a happy man [Collatinus]
JUNIUS: There goes a lucky man
TARQUINIUS: His fortune is worth more than my Etruscan
    crown
JUNIUS: But he is subject to your crown
TARQUINIUS: And I am subject to Lucretia.

—romantic panache, not lust! Tarquinius defends Lucretia against Junius's tensely delivered insinuations, and the climax of their exchange is Tarquinius's "I'll prove Lucretia chaste!"

The music returns to the "thirsty evening" that opened the scene and the Male Chorus describes the awakening of desire in Tarquinius's mind; the scene ends with the prince calling for his horse and leads straight into the Interlude— his Ride to Rome. It is remarkable that this scene is built around three low male voices—with the interpolations of the tenor Male Chorus—and is occupied exclusively with the masculinity of the characters; it is, however, imbued with the Lucretia motif.

The Ride to Rome is one of the most memorable passages of the opera. It is a peculiar aspect of *Lucretia* that Tarquinius's character is revealed more fully in the Male Chorus's commentary than in the music that Tarquinius himself sings. The Ride has this function: to portray the wholly animal Tarquinius, so closely identified with his horse that they become one:

EX. 15

It is, in fact, a metaphor aria in the tradition of Handel's
huntsmen Caesar, and Lucretia is portrayed, through metaphor and motif, in the River Tiber, which is conquered by
the horse. This image is recalled with a different sequel at
the moment of the rape: "Now the great river underneath
the ground/Flows through Lucretia, And Tarquinius is
drowned." Orchestrally it is an exciting *tour de force* in the
variety of textures achieved by the single instruments, from
the tutti-effect of the opening to the single flute which begins
the river section. Vocally it is no less magnificent, and it is
the most strongly characterised portrayal of Tarquinius in
the opera; indeed, in the last bar, at the climax of the phrase
quoted in Ex. 14 (this is its second appearance), a Bach-like
extension of the Lucretia motif occurs at Lucretia's name. It
is the very voice of Tarquinius we hear although it is sung by
the Male Chorus.

The second scene introduces the women, closely balancing
the first in its division into two parts—background information, and action germane to the plot. This scene divides at
the entry of Tarquinius. It also makes the same point of
introducing the characters in an activity which is, of itself,
characteristic—the drinking song in the generals' tent is
paralleled by the spinning ensemble in Lucretia's home.
There is a considerable contrast with the first scene, not only
the obvious contrasted pitch of the voices but in the pitch
and colour of the instruments: a different world is evoked in
the orchestra. The harp and woodwind are Lucretian instruments *par excellence*, just as strings, turgid or brilliant, and
drums are associated with the male characters. The spinning
ensemble is long, lyrical relief after the Ride. Action is re-
stored with the false alarm of an imagined knock at the door.
Lucretia's deeply passionate character is revealed more
quickly than Tarquinius's (there is probably more to reveal),
especially in this recitative and the aria fragment "How cruel
men are to teach us love". Perhaps alone among Britten's

major operatic characters (certainly in contrast with Grimes, Herring, Vere, Gloriana, the Governess and the Madwoman) Lucretia does not have a communications problem. Bianca understands her almost better than Lucretia does herself. Bianca and Lucia are the two facets of Lucretia—Bianca has the virtue without the passion, Lucia the passion without (we suspect) the virtue. Lucretia's character demonstrates how self-destructive this combination in one person is; but it does not isolate her from her women, although she disassociates herself from their less imaginative spheres of action. A second extended formal number ensues while the women fold linen —an essentially unpassionate and avowedly mundane occupation in which Lucretia does not vocally take part.

After the false alarm and the false (or psychological) lullaby of the linen ensemble, the Male and Female Choruses describe the real drama in interleaved fragments which coalesce as Tarquinius arrives. The characters mime the actions and reactions described by the choruses. The Tarquinius motif is conspicuous everywhere. The finale is a number involving all the characters—a "Goodnight" ensemble underlaid with the descending diminished fourth, full of foreboding. In this passage the characterisation is detailed —Lucretia's dignity, Bianca's "rude politeness at which a servant can excel", Lucia's self-conscious, eager feminity, firmly interrupted by the Male Chorus on behalf of Tarquinius (once more we feel these characters are, if momentarily, parallel).

The second act begins, like the first, with the Male and Female Choruses filling in the background of the Etruscan occupation, with off-stage Romans muttering revolt, and leading into a second statement of their Christian function. Although the chronological factor works the opposite way, this has the effect of a gradually focusing lens—from the contemporary Roman point of view the tragedy of Lucretia is minute, unimportant and even generally symptomatic of the

times; the Christian standpoint magnifies it to at least life
size. This immediately leads into the actual presence of
Lucretia—and the actual enacting of the tragedy.

The lyrical scene-setting music which we have now come to
expect at the beginning of a scene is on this occasion a lullaby
for the sleeping Lucretia. There is a most lovely and unusual
texture of sound, with alto flute, bass clarinet and muted
horn, which appears quite self-sufficient until the vocal line
appears above it:

EX. 16

(Unusual at this stage: low flutes and clarinets have also been
made significant in *Albert Herring*, the interlude of the second
act; *The Turn of the Screw*, Variation XI; *Gloriana*, the conspiracy scene in the second act, etc.) This music returns
intermittently up to the point when Tarquinius wakes
Lucretia—just as odd bars of the Ride to Rome recur until
Tarquinius arrives at Lucretia's home. It is first interrupted
by the description of Tarquinius's approach, an exciting passage of whispered (spoken) recitative accompanied by bass,
tenor and side drums and cymbals. The chorus speaks the
important words "The pity is that sin has so much grace It
moves like virtue"—both here and in the Ride to Rome I
feel the identification of the Male Chorus with Tarquinius to
be so close that it almost admits a grudging admiration on
the part of the Chorus for Tarquinius. Tarquinius is, anyway,
an un-villainly villain. The Ride to Rome is an almost heroic
piece. The libretto struggles to blacken his character by

(justifiable) aspersions on his horrifying ancestry and through the political and racial background of the opera: "Rome's for the Romans" and by implication "Roman women are for Roman men—only"! This all seems irrelevant to the Tarquinius we hear. Musically it is his "true Etruscan grace" that most often comes across.

Tarquinius reaches Lucretia's bed and sings an aria (his only aria in the opera), a *molto tranquillo* expression of a romantic aspiration; only the drum beats, brought forward from the Male Chorus's spoken recitative, belying his calm, Orestes-fashion. The melodic line of the aria is composed almost wholly of minor thirds and major sixths: Tarquinius "subject to Lucretia". This leads into an agitated version of the lullaby, with Tarquinius transforming the sleepy alto flute tune into an urgent "wake up, wake up, Lucretia" against which the Female Chorus contradicts him in her line from the lullaby.

When Lucretia wakes, a new tone colour, as well as a new tempo, announces the conflict—the cor anglais' weaving minor thirds against repeated brassed horn notes. The timpani beats, which have been important in presaging the climax, explode with Tarquinius's physical passion and diminished fourths dominate the melodic intervals in the orchestra. The words are full of echoes and predictions: Lucretia asks, "Is this is the Prince of Rome?" and Tarquinius, once "subject to Lucretia", now replies, "I am your prince"; Tarquinius cries, "Too late, Lucretia, too late", and we remember this when Collatinus later sings, "Too late, Junius, too late"—a hint of the theme of fate and inevitability that is sometimes indicated in the opera—Duncan wrote "Just as fertility or life is devoured by death, so is spirit defiled by Fate. Lucretia is, to my mind, the symbol of the former, Tarquinius the embodiment of the latter." I find that this theme makes the Christian exposition at the end of the opera irrelevant—the concept of fate excludes the concept of sin—and also helps to make

Tarquinius a less consistent character than if the opera came
down decisively either on the side of sin and redemption or
of fate (the triumph of circumstances over conscience).

The duet becomes an ensemble as the Male and Female
Choruses unite in urging, "Go, Tarquinius!" and the scene
ends with the third transformation of Ex. 14:

> See how the rampant centaur mounts the sky,
> And serves the sun, with all its seeds of stars,
> Now the great river underneath the ground,
> Flows through Lucretia, and Tarquinius is drowned.

The reason for Lucretia's submission is explicit in Obey and
Shakespeare—Tarquinius threatened to kill Lucretia and
"some rascal groom" and pretend to Collatinus that he had
killed Lucretia in her slave's embrace. This point is not made
in the opera, unless we are meant to read it into Tarquinius's
gesture with the sword. Without it, "The Seduction of
Lucretia" becomes a real alternative, which would, of course,
admit sin alongside fate: Lucretia's sin. The only textural
grounds for suspecting that Lucretia was ultimately a willing
victim is in the last scene; when she tells Collatinus that
Tarquinius "took his peace from me and *tore the fabric of our
love*", the orchestra recalls Tarquinius's accusation: "Yet the
linnet in your eyes lifts with desire, And the cherries of your
lips are wet with wanting." Were they? And does "deny"—
the most prominent word in Lucretia's answer—imply con-
tradiction (of a lie) or repudiation (of the truth)?

The interlude is a set of "chorale variations"; the Male
and Female Choruses, with the horn, have a hymn to the
Virgin against a stormy canonic accompaniment. The melodic
line of the hymn is, like the first hymn of the opera, derived
chiefly from the significant intervals of the opera—the minor
third and diminished fourth. Each variation relaxes the tension, as we move further away in time from the actual rape,
and the movement subsides into the second scene, "Lucretia's

home flooded with the early sun", with Bianca and Lucia arranging flowers. The scenes of women's mundane occupations—spinning, linen-folding, flower-arranging—contain the most resplendent music in the opera. No other state or activity is given such securely happy radiance of expression. This is a joyful relief after the tension of the night scene, and establishes again the norm of behaviour from which the principal characters deviate. The music is coloured predictably by the harp and abounds in the thirds characteristic of Lucretia. Lucretia's entry, by replacing aria with recitative, also replaces the bright harp and strings with the duller piano tone, and Lucretia's own phrases in an unusually low and restricted register answer the free, expansive arpeggios that Lucia and Bianca carry over from the preceding music.

From this point to the end of the passacaglia the music is continuously funereal—there are, in fact, three deaths, each separately mourned: the death of Lucretia's innocence, the death of her marriage, and the death of her body. *Lucretia* is a very contrived opera. The continuous use of the two motifs, for example, at times comes near to clogging the musical language with signposts to hidden significance, somewhat as the perpetual capitals and italics of eighteenth-century literature hinder the twentieth-century reader. There are passages, however, and this triple funeral is one, where we are grateful for the richness and detail of the working out.

Lucretia's essentially passionate nature turns to hysteria when she is offered orchids. In her outburst she sends a message to Collatinus:

> Tell the messenger to take my love. Yes! Give my love to the messenger, Give my love to the stable boy, and the coachman too. And hurry, hurry, For all men love the chaste Lucretia . . .

When Lucia goes out to send for Collatinus, the orchestra reminds us of the rape phrase and Lucretia sings a mourning

aria while she arranges the orchids into a wreath. This is the
funeral of her innocence and, to mark the contrast, Bianca
sings an aria recalling Lucretia's childhood, with the Lucretia
motif transformed into a *scherzando* accompaniment.

Collatinus arrives—too late to be intercepted by Bianca's
countermand of the summons; and Lucretia meets him—it
is the first time in the opera that we see them together—
while the orchestra plays a second dirge, a lament for the
death of their marriage:

EX. 17

Their reunion leads, through an intense, beautiful and impassioned dialogue, to Lucretia's inevitable suicide*—inevitable
for her because of her shame which feels like sin and demands
atonement, inevitable in the eyes of the characters on stage
because "to love as [they] loved was to be Never but as
moiety" and when Lucretia's chastity was despoiled, her
marriage and even her life had to end; inevitable for the
audience because they have already seen the wreath and
heard the funeral march.

There follows the third funeral—an actual funeral march
which is a passacaglia based on a theme closely derived from
the "framing hymn" of the Male and Female Choruses. The

* In the only production I have seen of this, Lucretia stabs herself with
Junius's sword, which seems an excellent idea—he is the instrument of
the tragedy throughout.

Choruses have not taken part in the scene up to this point—
an unusually long absence from the score—as if they used up
their powers in willing the tragedy not to take place, and can
only watch the second tragedy, exhausted of comment, until
they gather up the themes of the opera in their final passage.
The passacaglia gradually introduces all the living characters
(except Tarquinius—and he is omitted not only for practical
reasons; like Essex towards the end of *Gloriana*, he is withdrawn from a prominence which might contest the central
role) in characteristic lines: Collatinus mourning over
Lucretia's body ("So brief is beauty—is this it all?"), Junius
already haranguing the crowd from the window ("Romans,
arise, see what the Etruscans have done"), Lucia and Bianca
share an entry in "feminine" thirds ("Now place the wreath
about her head . . ."). The Female Chorus enters the ensemble next, very brilliantly above the accumulating melodic
lines, and finally the Male Chorus dominates the ensemble.
Through the various strands of the voice parts the bass theme
is given some key verbal meanings—the scale passage is
identified with "So brief is beauty"; the rising third with the
question "is this it all?" and the falling third with "it is all":

EX. 18

So   brief___ is   beau-ty!   Is this it all?   It   is   all!

The passacaglia, then, gathers together the pagan tragedy,
musically, poetically and dramatically. At the climax the
voices sing in unison moving towards the question and answer
quoted above. The scale is extended up through the orchestra
("beauty" becoming less "brief"?) and the Female Chorus
sings, accompanied only by the "question" phrase, a questioning passage: "Is all this suffering and pain, is this in vain?"
This is answered in a splendid arioso by the Male Chorus
where the melodic line gradually incorporates all the signi-

ficant motifs, culminating in the "answer" when Christ's forgiveness is mentioned, from which point to the end the falling third—the answer—dominates the orchestral writing. The
Male and Female Choruses sing their hymn for the last time.

It seems to me that the Male Chorus's answer—

It is not all . . .
Though our nature's still as frail
And we still fall
and that great crowd's no less along that road,
endless and uphill.
For now He bears our sin
and does not fall,
and He carrying all turns round
stoned with our doubt
and then forgives us all . . .

—while immensely right-feeling in performance, is somewhat
irrelevant to the drama when examined in cold blood. It is
about sin: now the only sin we have indisputably met with
in the opera is on the part of Junius and Tarquinius; surely
the least pressing need at this stage in the drama is a desire
for Junius or Tarquinius to be forgiven. It is about forgiveness: if, as seems more reasonable dramatically, it intends to
say that Christian forgiveness would have rendered Lucretia's
suicide unnecessary, then we have to remember that Lucretia
has not sinned in a Christian sense, so no forgiveness is necessary. In any case, Lucretia's death, a Stoic death, is unnecessary even in her own age after Collatinus, anachronistically
enlightened, has forgiven "what Lucretia has given". It is
here that the ambivalence of the opera's motivation is most
unsatisfactory—whether it is about the workings of fate in a
pagan society or about the operation of Grace among redeemed men and women.

The opera is dominated structurally and dramatically by
its use of the two motifs. I haven't mentioned more than a

few key uses of these because there are more bars in the opera that have some derivation from them, than bars that have not. Most of the uses are conspicuous, easily perceptible by an audience which has not seen the work before. These fulfil a potent dramatic purpose, as when in the first scene Lucretia's name—and motif—is bandied about until Junius's outburst seems both inevitable and easily comprehensible. Just as clearly Tarquinius's theme provides a heavy and ominous accompaniment to the "Good night" ensemble. The verbal meanings progressively attached to the three phrases of the passacaglia bass have already been shown. It is a very verbal opera. There is no single piece of instrumental music that does not later become part of a vocal one (the lullaby in Act II, Scene 1 and the "funeral" music when Lucretia meets Collatinus in the last scene hold their independence for longer than any others). The motif system seems in this opera to be an extension of this wordyness: to drive home the metaphor of the horse and the river, in Tarquinius's Ride, the flute and viola shout "Lucretia" in every bar; when Collatinus asks Bianca if Tarquinius has been to his house, she tells him so in the notes she sings although she refuses to do so in words. They are melodic motifs—Lucretia's is almost a tune—and are developed melodically for the most part, which makes their perception easier. Indeed, unless they are perceptible to the audience which has not seen the score, they are irrelevant to the audience which is likely to be watching the opera (though not to the composer); from this point of view Britten's use of them is an unqualified success.

But the most exciting aspect of the opera is the vast range of instrumental sonorities resulting from the chamber forces. We are far more aware of the orchestra in this opera—with its absence of instrumental passages—than in many a full-scale work, including *Peter Grimes*. The individual colouring of each passage is usually created by the use of even smaller ensembles from the group. This allows the unusual sounds produced by the alto flute, bass clarinet, and high bassoon register, for example, to be readily appreciated. The cor anglais gradually emerges from the "middle funeral" movement to confront Lucretia (in an unaccompanied duet with her) with the very voice of her sorrow. The viola and cello duet with the flute, later clarinet, in the flower scene creates a sound as brilliant as the sunlight which is dominating the stage. The harp is the most versatile member of the ensemble: its music ranges from the chirping cricket in the oppressive heat in the first scene to the enchanting spinning ensemble.

There is nothing groping or experimental in Britten's use of the medium he devised for *Lucretia*; we do not even feel it to be a limitation: it is rather a revelation of the added scope such a refinement of style and means brings to the interpretation of the drama.

Chapter three

Albert Herring

Libretto by Eric Crozier from a short story, *Le Rosier de Madame Husson* (1888), by Maupassant.
First performed Glyndebourne, June 1947.

CHARACTERS

LADY BILLOWS, an elderly autocrat	Joan Cross, *soprano*
FLORENCE PIKE, her housekeeper and companion	Gladys Parr, *contralto*
MISS WORDSWORTH, schoolmistress	Margaret Ritchie, *soprano*
MR GEDGE, the Vicar	William Parsons, *baritone*
MR UPFOLD, the Mayor	Roy Ashton, *tenor*
SUPERINTENDENT BUDD, police super-intendent	{ Norman Lumsden, *bass* { Bruce Clark
SID, a butcher's shophand	{ Frederick Sharp, *baritone* { Denis Dowling
ALBERT HERRING, from the green-grocer's	Peter Pears, *tenor*
NANCY, from the bakery	{ Nancy Evans, *mezzo-soprano* { Joan Gray
MRS HERRING, Albert's mother	{ Betsy de la Porte, *mezzo-soprano* { Catherine Lawson
EMMIE	Lesley Duff, *soprano*
CIS } village children	{ Anne Sharp, *soprano* { Elisabeth Parry
HARRY	David Spenser, *treble*

Conductors: Benjamin Britten, Ivan Clayton
Producer: Frederick Ashton
Scenery and Costumes: John Piper

The story takes place at Loxford, a small market town in East Suffolk, during April and May of 1900.

ACT I, SCENE I: Lady Billows's house. Lady Billows is anxious to revive the May Day celebrations she remembers from her childhood, and to raise the moral standards of the village. She summons a Committee to elect a May Queen. None of the suggested candidates stands up to the scrutiny of Florence Pike, her housekeeper. In desperation Superintendent Budd proposes a May King in the person of Albert Herring, a slightly simple but undeniably virtuous village youth.

SCENE 2: In their greengrocery store, Albert and his mother are informed of the celebrations—and the £25 prize. Albert attempts rebellion, but is firmly quelled by his mother.

ACT II, SCENE I: Inside a marquee. In the last-minute preparations for the festival Sid and Nancy, Albert's friends, bent on promoting his emancipation, put rum in Albert's lemonade. The welcome ode, speeches, and toast go more or less as planned. Albert is thoroughly miserable until he has tasted the lemonade—which cheers him considerably!

SCENE 2: Albert returns home to the shop after the Festival, having enjoyed himself. His restless desires are rekindled when he overhears Sid and Nancy discussing him in the street. He remembers his prize money and decides by the toss of a coin to go out in search of adventure. Mrs Herring returns and, thinking Albert is already asleep, retires to bed.

ACT III : The shop, the following day. Albert has disappeared and various amateur search parties are out in pursuit. His orange-blossom crown is brought in, battered and bespattered, and taking this as the embodiment of Albert, the company assemble around it and sing a tragic-comic lament. Albert enters and their grief changes to an unfriendly inquisition. Albert reveals "a general sample" of his debauchery ("it wasn't much fun") and with growing confidence sends his neighbours about their business.

Albert Herring was first performed in June 1947, Britten's second chamber opera. It deals as lightly with the theme of chastity as *Lucretia* dealt tragically. The libretto derives from a short story by Maupassant, *Le Rosier de Madame Husson*, which is a grim tale in the original version. In *Albert Herring* it has been transformed into an opera which is not only comic but funny. And there is inevitably some uneasiness in the transformation, for it is difficult to find a consistent dramatic purpose in *Albert Herring*. It veers between caricature and comedy, and while the caricature roles are for the most part quite brilliantly presented, we are left with an unsatisfying human comedy which is perhaps necessarily inconclusive but also disturbingly inconsistent. Sid's seductive picture, for example, of the pleasures of love ("Girl's mean Spring six days a week") is one of the high points in the opera—as music and as musical characterisation—but this glowing evocation is irrelevant to the freedom that Albert goes after in his "night that was a nightmare example of drunkenness, dirt and worse", and nothing in his "liberated" character in the last scene leads us to imagine that he could ever achieve it. The puritan confusion which enabled the inhabitants of Loxford to identify love and drunkenness as being sins of a kind seems also to have confused the composer and librettist.

Albert is not an easy character to portray. As usual, Britten gives him a musical character which is easier to understand—and like—than his verbal character. Is he really emancipated at the end of the opera? Was it worth the small orgy and, perhaps more important, the Threnody, to emerge as the Albert of the last scene? Only in terms of his musical character can we answer unequivocally yes—in terms of the sequence of numbers, "It seems as clear as clear can be" (Ex. 21), "The tide will turn, the sun will set" (Ex. 24) and "And I'm more than grateful to you all" (Ex. 26). In this last confident, capable passage Albert has achieved self-possession—literally, he now "possesses" himself. But how this resulted from the events of the previous night it is difficult to guess.

The first scene is the most satisfying in the opera. Dealing only with the caricature characters, it has a balance and consistency which is lacking in the rest of the opera, as well as containing most of the intrinsically musical humour—in contrast to verbal or musically allusive humour which is rampant elsewhere. It opens with a brisk, perpetual-motion orchestral pattern, which includes semitone "sighing" phrases without impeding the movement and incorporates Florence's aria as well as her conversation with Lady Billows. It extends until the arrival of the Committee. Comic opera tends to generate extended instrumental forms: the music has to depict and accompany situations rather than the protagonists' introspections. Whether it is to depict a scene, as this opening section portrays the incessant activity urged on Florence Pike, or to accompany a situation, like the waltz which points the performing-animal aspect of the Committee members' reports, the instrumental music generally has to bind together comparatively undeveloped vocal lines, and establish the musical dimension of the scene.

The disorganised inanities of the arriving Committee members are delivered in recitative (over piano chords—the only occasions on which the accompaniment deviates from this are significant: the clock chiming the half-hour, which provokes conventional reactions from the Superintendent and the Mayor—it returns, incidentally, at the crisis of the opera, Albert's decision to break loose at the end of the second act— the flowing arpeggios which accompany Miss Wordsworth's lyrical excesses, and the solemn octaves which give indisputable authority to "In like a lion, out like a lamb"). The second musical unit begins with the entry of Lady Billows: organisation rears its formidable head, and this change is

reflected in the form of the music. The material is threefold—
the double-dotted slow march, the posture of authority; the
repeated chords, submissive and unanimous reaction; and the
fugue—the cause of bringing the two former ideas together is
reflected in its purposeful, busy, and contrived effect. These
impressions are confirmed when the march returns to accompany the "Good mornings", the repeated chords, the
agenda—

> This is the tenth of April,
> The day your Ladyship planned
> For our second and final meeting—
> We're here to see how we stand . . .

and the fugue (complete with cadential trill) becomes "We've
made our own investigations", conveying the self-importance
of the singers and of the procedural routine of the meeting.

Lady Billows's forceful brand of lyricism provides some
contrast to this, though in her aria "May Queen, May Queen"
the orchestra continues to refer to the investigations in a
scherzando version of the fugue subject. The *recitativo quasi
ballata* which follows is a substantial ensemble, with suggestions proposed to a confident, major-key phrase, invariably
refuted by Florence with a change to the minor and energetic-
ally turned down by Lady Billows:

EX. 19

When all the suggestions are exhausted, the first phrase, now in the minor, becomes a lament, for Miss Wordsworth, the Mayor, the Vicar, and Superintendent Budd. It is interrupted by a genuinely sad and angry aria for Lady Billows which lifts her momentarily out of the caricature class, to a place among the real people of the opera. It is amusing, of course, because its energy is disproportionate to Florence's insubstantial allegations, but it is none the less moving, as a deeply felt, if misguided, reaction. The Threnody in the last act is a similar case—it is, quite simply, funny to see the cast assemble round the battered orange-blossom crown and treat it as if it were a corpse. But their inflated emotions are real enough to them and are accorded sympathetic musical expression which, because their grief is disproportionate, if not inappropriate, makes for a musical number which is dramatically disproportionate and possibly dramatically inappropriate, too.

Albert Herring is proposed as May King: the phrase in which the amazed Committee react to the outrageous suggestion becomes, freely varied, the basis of the Superintendent's short air "Albert Herring's clean as new-mown hay". Lady Billows is not impressed and casts desperately around for alternatives, but Florence's minor-key version of Ex. 19 ("Country virgins, if there be such, think too little and see too much") has a damning finality that Lady Billows cannot overcome; she is defeated by her own vigilance, which has doubtless schooled Florence into an attitude of universal suspicion. She is, however, reluctant to abandon the festival

and turns to the Vicar, less for moral enlightenment, more
for reassurance, from the only member of the Committee of
comparable social status, that she will not be making a fool
of herself if she awards the prize to Albert. It is the occasion
of an enchanting short air for the Vicar, depicting his hesitant
lyricism. Now we can make a contrast between this and Miss
Wordsworth's too-fluent, eager lyrical style: at the beginning
of the scene these two were aligned against the considerably
less articulate Mayor and Budd. The detailed characterisation in the brief arias is particularly important because in the
ensembles in this scene the characters either sing the same
words or the same notes: it is the unanimity of their approach
to the investigations or reaction to the creation of a May King
that is pertinent.

In the face of the inescapable fact of Albert's virtue, Lady
Billows capitulates and her enthusiasm for the idea now equals
her previous distaste: "Right! We'll have him! May King!
That'll teach the girls a lesson!" This is the starting-point for
the finale: a rousing fugue (the head of the subject,

EX. 20

May   King!   May   King!

being the same phrase which opened Lady Billow's earlier,
vehemently nostalgic aria "May Queen") and a concerto-
like coda with extravagantly brilliant phrases for Lady Billows
set against meek, if *fortissimo*, responses by the Committee. It
dissolves into the interlude which is underlaid by the bounc-
ing ball rhythm—we realise that this is what is being represented at the opening of the next scene.

This scene attempts to portray the inhibited Albert—
Albert in need of rescue. He is therefore shown in contrast to
the entirely spontaneous though unattractive children and
the hedonistic Sid and Nancy—a very sound picture of normal
love among the misfits and exaggerations of the rest of the

c

characters. More weighty evidence on the side of the rescuers
is revealed when Mrs Herring appears. And the crowning
absurdity of Lady Billows's procession shows Albert out-
numbered and outraged—he is sure of our sympathy from
this point onwards. The central statement of his musical
character is:

EX. 21

This is the "simple" Albert, harmonically pallid in comparison with the rich chord change suggested by "Sid's ideas"
and rhythmically limited after:

EX. 22

Yet with enough potential—he does, after all, realise his predicament, and this is a very beautiful and passionate aria —to make his development likely and worthwhile. It is typical of Albert's lot that this soliloquy is twice interrupted. The procession has the immediate effect of jerking Albert out of his predominantly scale-wise melodic intervals: "Concerns me, do you say!" leaps a major sixth and "What! Me?" an octave. The procession is stylised, like the Committee suggestions and resolution in the first scene, and the festival song and toast in the next act—a rigid *marziale* utterance by Lady Billows—utterly ridiculous in content and context. When "Mum" is won over by the £25 prize, Albert is indeed a hunted man.

Act II, Scene 1 is farce—it is the situation which is paramount. The characters are all at their most exaggerated and the drama relies heavily on allusive rather than intrinsic humour. It is all very funny—the nightmare rehearsal, the quotation from *Tristan*, the speeches—but it contributes nothing to the development of the characters and little to the plot. It is not the turning-point for Albert—that comes in the following scene. The act opens with a horn fanfare, extending the "May King" phrase of Ex. 20, set against restless, bustling semiquaver movement; this becomes identified with the preparations for the festival when it forms part of Florence's aria "For three precious weeks . . ." Miss Wordsworth rehearses the "festive song". The episode is unworthy of her—she is, admittedly, sillier than Ellen Orford, and less perceptive than the Governess, but she is basically of the same mould and is in some way betrayed by this scene. The children, too, are a miscalculation. Children cannot be caricatured graphically, and this attempt to distort them musically is embarrassing— particularly among the many splendid operatic children Britten has created.

The cast assembles to fragments of their earlier music. Sid pours rum into Albert's glass accompanied by a reference to the Love Potion from *Tristan*. The speeches are delivered in characteristic manner—Lady Billows's didactic patriotism, the Mayor's civic trivia, Miss Wordsworth's exuberant innocence and Superintendent Budd's inefficient bumbling (this latter accompanied by an energetic double bass solo). Albert's agonised embarrassment contrasts with the varied brands of confidence exhibited in the speeches:

EX. 23

The toast follows, another organised number, the musical process reflecting the self-consciousness of the characters singing, and when Albert drinks his fortified lemonade the *Tristan* chord runs riot through the orchestra and recurs irreverently to accompany his hiccups.

The music of the toast and the mood of festive euphoria continue into the interlude till it subsides in a lovely meditation for alto flute and bass clarinet—apparently depicting the inward-looking Albert we see at the end of the next scene. But when this music returns in Scene 2 it is to accompany his clowning: "we'll light the gas, With enormous care not to break the mantle, Set fire to the shop or cause a scandal!"

Albert is already considerably more self-confident than in Act
I, and he is happy enough until he overhears Sid and Nancy's
meeting in the street. His regret turns first to bitterness, next
to this moving statement:

EX. 24

The high seriousness of this passage is questionable characterisation: anyone capable of expressing his thoughts through it
should not need emancipation by orgy. Albert's musical
character is at times on a different plane from his dramatic
character—perhaps necessarily here, for he has to provide a
musical climax for the scene that will efface the memory of
Sid and Nancy's passionate duets. The alto flute and bass
clarinet music returns to see Mrs Herring safely into bed and
to close the scene on the catalystic night.

The third act continues to illustrate the ridiculous elements
in Loxford daily life. And for the first time Albert is not included in the ridicule. The introduction evokes the confusion
of the search in rising and falling arpeggio shapes pervaded
by the | ♪ ♩ ♩ ♪| rhythm, first announced on the side drum.
This pattern continues intermittently in the scene until the
Threnody, and returns, when Albert appears, for the chorus
"Tearing the town from its regular labours". The disorganised
nature of the search is indicated by a series of interrupted
glimpses of the search parties, from the "Peewit Patrol" to
the "Wickham Market Militia". Nancy and Mrs Herring are
fixed points against the disrupting background activity.
Nancy's remorse and Mrs Herring's grief are genuine, if
sentimental, and are communicated in a dispassionate chro-
maticism which registers their distress without enlisting a
strenuous sympathy from the audience:

EX. 25

The procession which brings in the orange-blossom crown (". . . on a tray covered with a white cloth . . . lying there —crushed and muddied") parallels Lady Billows's procession in Act I, Scene 2. In contrast to the disorganised procedure of the search parties (and consistent with the superfluous formalities of the Committee scene, the announcing of the award of the prize to Albert, the festival song and toast), it is predictable that the mass mourning over the "wreath" and its implications should take place in a formal number, the Threnody—a choral lament over a ground bass with solo verses for each character, culminating in the simultaneous statement of all the solos. It is not an easy number to absorb into the opera. It balances on a knife-edge of taste and it is a matter of opinion as to whether it dangerously inclines towards being too funny about death or being too tragic for both the ludicrous circumstances and the light-hearted mood of the rest of the opera. The problematic factor is its length (dictated to a large extent by the form: each of the nine soloists must have a solo verse) which forces the listener to come to a decision about it. It is perhaps justified by being dramatically true: this is the way these characters would behave, their grief would be eloquent and disproportionate and provoked by insufficient evidence. But until this point in the opera they have for the most part been treated as caricatures, and deprived of the sort of rounded portrayal which would entitle them to pathos.

It breaks up, anyway, in unambiguous comedy—the falling minor ninths of "and die so young" are turned into a rising major ninth for the astonished cry of "Albert?" as he reappears. It is splendid comedy, too, when they continue the chordal style of the Threnody into their furious and unwelcoming

> Where have you come from?
> Where have you been?
> Wrecking the whole of our daily routine?

Albert is at first silenced by their vehemence but eventually narrates a "general sample" of his experiments—in an experimental style, too, for Albert, though a restless and uneasy one.

These experiences are not assimilated—or perhaps it is not the night's adventures but the act of speaking his mind to the assembled company that is the turning-point—until the line:

EX. 26

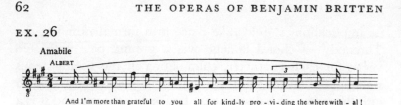

And I'm more than grateful to you all for kind-ly pro - vi - ding the wherewith - al!

This is the sequel to Ex. 21 and Ex. 24; Albert's musical characterisation is completed when it has been stated not once but three times (ending always on a different chord), undisturbed by the abuse of all except Sid and Nancy. The minor characters who swelled in a nightmarish fantasy to dominate the stage during the Threnody now diminish to silhouettes and are dismissed by Albert—who, we now feel, will be able to keep them in their proper place. But this is all. He is as far removed as ever from the romantic ideal that prompted his earlier dreams and eventual escape. Of course, this, like the Threnody, is real life: but reality is not a satisfying note on which to end a period satire.

Chapter four

The Little Sweep

Libretto by Eric Crozier.
First performed Jubilee Hall, Aldeburgh, 1949.

CHARACTERS

BLACK BOB, the sweepmaster	{ Norman Lumsden, *bass* { John Highcock
CLEM, his assistant	{ Max Worthley, *tenor* { Andrew Gold
SAM, their sweepboy	{ John Moules, *treble* { Alan Woolston
MISS BAGGOTT, the housekeeper	{ Gladys Parr, *contralto* { Anne Wood
ROWAN, the nursery maid	{ Elisabeth Parry, *soprano* { Pamela Woolmore
JULIET BROOK	Anne Sharp, *soprano*
GAY BROOK	{ Bruce Hines, *treble* { Michael Nicholls
SOPHIE BROOK	{ Monica Garrod, *soprano* { Jean Galton
JOHNNIE CROME	{ Peter Cousins, *treble* { Brian Cole
HUGH CROME	{ Ralph Canham, *treble* { Clive Wyatt
TINA CROME	{ Mavis Gardiner, *soprano* { Shirley Eaton

JULIET BROOK, GAY BROOK, SOPHIE BROOK } the children

JOHNNIE CROME, HUGH CROME, TINA CROME } their cousins

Conductors: Norman del Mar, Trevor Harvey
Producers: Basil Coleman, Stuart Burge
Scenery and Costumes: John Lewis

Black Bob and Clem, chimney-sweeps, arrive at Iken Hall with their new sweepboy, Sam. The three children who live at Iken, Juliet, Gay, and Sophie, and their three cousins who are staying with them, Johnnie, Hugh, and Tina, are playing hide-and-seek. They hear Sam's cries for help when he is stuck in the nursery chimney and succeed in pulling him down again. They are concerned at his plight and in order to save him from his masters they lay a false trail of sooty foot-prints leading to the window, and hide Sam in their toy cupboard. Black Bob, Clem, and the housekeeper, Miss Baggott, are deceived and set off in pursuit of the false trail. Rowan, the nursery maid, thinking that Sam is indeed being pursued, expresses her pity for him, and the children take advantage of these emotions which they overhear to present her with the *fait accompli* of the rescued Sam. They bath him and plan to send him back to his parents, who live near the cousins' home.

Miss Baggott returns sooner than expected and all but discovers Sam; Juliet, however, creates a diversion by pre-tending to faint. The next morning Sam is hidden in the trunk ready to be taken home with the departing cousins. There is nearly a last-minute tragedy when the coachman and the gardener, arriving to remove the trunk, declare it is too heavy to be moved, and must be unpacked! The children, however, offer to help, and Sam is borne away to safety.

The Little Sweep was first performed in June 1949 as the culmination of the entertainment *Let's Make an Opera*, by Eric Crozier. This work, designed for children and with a large proportion of child singers, takes its place both among the considerable volume of children's music Britten has written, and, rather surprisingly with complete consistency among his operas for adults. The instrumental forces are smaller than in the preceding chamber operas—string quartet, piano duet, and percussion. They are somewhat extended by the vast choir formed by the audience, which is rehearsed in the earlier part of the entertainment and is responsible for the introduction, interludes, and finale of the actual opera. The work is, then, a very involving experience, and although it has no pretensions to be didactic, no one can emerge from it without having a clearer idea of the raw material of opera and indeed of music itself.

Like most of Britten's operas, it is concerned with suffering and oppression. The villain—Black Bob—is all the more villainous for being briefly sketched: the more fully Britten portrays evil, the more sympathetic it usually becomes—this happens with Tarquinius and Claggart and has begun to happen before the opera begins with Peter Grimes. There are no concessions to the young performers and audience in the portrayal of the terrible facts of child chimney-sweeps. The brutality is not implied, it is demonstrated. However, it is shown to come only tangentially into contact with the children's world (I am not including Sam in their world: he is far too experienced to be counted as a child) and it is vanquished by their gaiety and resourcefulness. The children have their own domestic villain, Miss Baggott—she has some very sadistic lines—but she holds no terror because she is familiar, and leaves no uneasiness because she becomes a comic character.

The children are not direct witnesses of brutality, but they are brought face to face with suffering. This is reflected in the scope of their music, which contains, apart from the exuberant Shanty and Marching song, the range of grief expressed in the ensembles: "Is he wounded? Please forgive us"—their spontaneous distress when Sam falls down the chimney; the very much more detached and philosophical "O why do you weep through the working day"—where the children actually put themselves in Sam's place and make his answers for him; and the stylised imitation of grief, "Poor Juliet's ill! Look how she's lying". This range is further extended by Rowan's music: she is the adult mouthpiece of the children and has all their responsiveness and sensibility with, in addition, the power to act on it.

The first number, which involves the audience, Black Bob, and Clem, is "The Sweep's Song"—the opening cry of

EX. 27

Sweep!____

introduces immediately the rasp of physical cruelty, and is followed by a forward-moving $\frac{5}{4}$ tune. All of Britten's operas have a satisfying proportion of "take home" tunes and the works involving children are particularly abundant in these. Naturally the audience songs contain material which it is easy to memorise. There is scarcely an aria in the whole of this opera and very little solo music; the audience songs provide instead the melodic climaxes.

Most of the numbers are ensembles. In the next, we are shown three inflexible adults striking characteristic attitudes, in contrast with which Rowan appears an infinitely more real person, and in consequence has a more developed musical style through which to express her maturity. Black Bob and

Clem are examples of the "we have always done it this way" motivation (exactly the same force which brings about the tragedy in *Billy Budd*)—

> Chimney-sweepers must 'ave boys,
> Same as poachers must 'ave ferrets.
> Brushes, rods and such like toys
> Can't compete with human merits.

Miss Baggott's operatic antecedents are geographically nearer —Mrs Sedley (*Peter Grimes*) and Florence Pike (*Albert Herring*). The duet which follows, "Now little white boy", over a lashing ground bass not so very far removed from the viola theme of Interlude IV in *Peter Grimes*, gives full expression to the sadism of the sweeps. At the end of the duet Sam is up the chimney and an instrumental reference to Rowan's pitying line in the previous quartet makes its poignant comment.

The children are introduced vocally off-stage in a game of hide-and-seek: this is interrupted by Sam's cries—he is stuck in the chimney—and they pull him down while they sing a Shanty. His grief and theirs is expressed in traditionally chromatic language:

EX. 28

They hide Sam in their toy cupboard after leaving

> Sooty tracks upon the sheet,
> Sooty marks of sooty feet,

> Soot upon the window seat
> Make our evidence complete.

This is amusingly parodied by Miss Baggott, Clem, and Bob
(cruelty is less frightening when it can be outwitted), who are
deceived by the false trail and hurry in pursuit to a vigorous
and bloodthirsty trio: "Wait until we catch him, We'll whip
him till he howls!"

Again Rowan is shown to be more fully human, as well as
humanitarian, in contrast to the slightly caricatured villains.
She has a sophisticated accompanied recitative, "Run, poor
sweepboy", which is not less moving for depicting an escape
that Sam has not made. The children identify themselves
with Rowan when they interrupt her in similar style and
organise her sympathy into practical help with "Sammy's
Bath"—another audience song, which bridges the two
scenes.

The swinging hemiola rhythm of the Bath song is transformed in the next ensemble into a pathetic statement of pain
that cannot be dealt with as easily as the soot: "O why do
you weep through the working day" is the emotional climax
of the opera. It is a reasoned acknowledgement, almost an
acceptance, of suffering, more mature than the children's first
indignant reaction; a statement which is continuously relevant, at the beginning and at the end of the opera:

EX. 29

The mood is quickly dissolved in action. Miss Baggott
returns (a parody of the pathetic semitones at "Oh! my poor
feet!"—Britten ensures that the audience learns all the tricks!)
and attempts to open the toy cupboard in which Sam is
again hiding. Juliet saves the situation by a mock faint which
sets in motion the scene finale—a splendid passacaglia over
a rising scale with the pretended emotions of Rowan and the
children clearly differentiated from their normal styles
(Rowan's line is almost colourless, the children's deadpan
and lifeless) and Miss Baggott's genuine flurry just as plainly
in character.

The third audience song, "The Night Song", covers the

lapse of time between the close of the second scene and the opening of the third: it is not connected directly with the plot and its function is to evoke the night and provide relaxation after the excitements of the second scene finale. This it does in a lovely and expansive tune which gives the audience the experience of taking part in building a big climax of sound and letting it die away. The long, lyrical phrases of the audience songs are especially welcome in contrast to the short vocal lines of the children: Juliet's aria "Soon the coach will carry you away", which follows this, shows the short phrases built into quite an extended solo for the proportions of this work. The long phrases of the string quartet give it the illusion of being a broader utterance.

After a comic altercation with the coachman and the gardener (usually Black Bob and Clem, not too heavily disguised, which removes, in an extra-dramatic way, any lingering nightmares from the initial cruelty of the opera) the trunk containing Sam is dispatched with the parting children. Realism recedes as the finale is staged—for the fourth audience song, "the whole cast has come quickly back on stage. They improvise a coach with the trunk, rocking horse and a chair or two. The Twins kneel, twirling parasoles, Sam rides the horse and Tom flourishes a whip." It is an effective way of saying that art can be as artificial as you like; drama is not less true for having its construction exposed.

Indeed, this is what the whole entertainment is about. Participation is made easy in *The Little Sweep*, but it is intended to be carried forward—as involvement—in our appreciation of all Britten's operas: all levels to be attempted!

Chapter five

Billy Budd

Libretto by E. M. Forster and Eric Crozier from the story of the same name (1891) by Herman Melville.
First performed Covent Garden, December 1951.

CHARACTERS

EDWARD FAIRFAX VERE, Captain of H.M.S. *Indomitable*	Peter Pears, *tenor*
BILLY BUDD, able seamen	Theodore Uppman, *baritone*
JOHN CLAGGART, the Master-at-Arms	Frederick Dalberg, *bass*
MR REDBURN, the First Lieutenant	Hervey Alan, *baritone*
MR FLINT, the Sailing Master	Gervaint Evans, *bass baritone*
MR RATCLIFFE, the Second Lieutenant	Michael Langdon, *bass*
RED WHISKERS, an impressed man	Anthony Marlowe, *tenor*
DONALD, a sailor	Bryan Drake, *baritone*
DANSKER, an old seaman	Inia Te Wiata, *bass*
A NOVICE	William McAlpine, *tenor*
SQUEAK, a ship's corporal	David Tree, *tenor*
BOSUN	Ronald Lewis, *baritone*
FIRST MATE	Rhydderch Davies, *baritone*
SECOND MATE	Hubert Littlewood, *baritone*
MAINTOP	Emlyn Jones, *tenor*
NOVICE'S FRIEND	John Cameron, *baritone*
ARTHUR JONES, an impressed man	Alan Hobson, *baritone*
FOUR MIDSHIPMEN	Brian Ettridge, Kenneth Nash, Peter Spencer, Colin Waller, *boy's voices*
CABIN BOY	Peter Flynn, *spoken*

Conductor: Benjamin Britten
Producer: Basil Coleman
Designer: John Piper
Chorus Master: Douglas Robinson

The story takes place on board H.M.S. *Indomitable*, a seventy-four, during the French wars of 1797.

PROLOGUE: Captain Vere, as an old man looks back on his life at sea and recalls with difficulty some confusing incident from "the summer of seventeen hundred and ninety seven" which he feels to have had some spiritual impact on him.

ACT I, SCENE 1: Early morning on H.M.S. *Indomitable*, the daily work goes forward. A boarding party returns from a passing merchantman, *The Rights o' Man*; three men have been impressed and they are brought before the officers. One of them is Billy Budd, a young seaman of outstanding physical presence and spiritual innocence. His only defect is an occasional stammer. He arouses an ambiguous response from the Master-at-Arms, John Claggart, who commends Billy's virtues to his superior officers, while ordering his corporal, Squeak, to provoke Billy's temper.

SCENE 2: Captain Vere's cabin; evening, a week later. The ship is approaching enemy waters and both the officers and men are eager for action. The officers confess their fears of mutiny—the revolts at the Spithead and the Nore have only recently been concluded—and establish extra vigilance to defeat it.

SCENE 3: The berth deck, the same evening. The men are singing shanties. Billy discovers Squeak interfering with his kit and attacks him, knocking him down just as Claggart appears. Claggart again behaves ambiguously. He has

Squeak—who was carrying out his orders—arrested, and commends Billy :"Handsomely done, my lad. And handsome is as handsome did it, too." Subsequently, in a soliloquy he plans Billy's destruction. He employs the Novice, whose spirit has been broken by a brutal flogging and who will now do anything to avoid another one, to attempt to bribe Billy to lead a mutiny. The Novice unwillingly does this, but arouses only Billy's rage and his stammer.

ACT II, SCENE I : The main deck and quarter-deck some days later. The men are spoiling for battle and are continually frustrated by a thick sea mist. Claggart begins to put his case against Billy to Captain Vere, but is interrupted when a French sail is sighted and the mist begins to lift. There are exciting preparations and a shot is fired, but it falls short; the wind drops and the mist returns to put an end to the chase. Claggart comes to Vere again with his tale of Billy's intended mutiny. Vere refuses to believe him, but immediately arranges a confrontation.

SCENE 2: Vere, in his cabin a few minutes later, is confident of Billy's innocence. Billy is brought in and protests his loyalty. Claggart makes his accusation which renders Billy speechless. His stammer chokes him and he hits out at Claggart and strikes him dead. Vere summons his officers, realising only after he has acted that Billy is unalterably good and that it will fall to him, Vere, to see that Billy is condemned. He summons a drumhead court at which the officers, frustrated by the lack of guidance from Vere and directed by the urgency of the situation in a time of war, condemn Billy to death. Vere accepts their verdict and personally reveals it to Billy.

SCENE 3: A bay of the gun deck, shortly before dawn the next morning. Billy is in irons; he is visited by Dansker and refuses

to encourage the threatened mutiny. He blesses Captain Vere
and is hanged.

EPILOGUE : Vere, as an old man, looking back to the incident,
remembers Billy's blessing and is comforted.

Billy Budd was first performed in December 1951, the second of Britten's full-scale operas. The libretto is by E. M. Forster and Eric Crozier, from the novel by Herman Melville. At that time it must have seemed an enormous development from its predecessors and it remains one of Britten's biggest operas in a number of senses. In comparison with the only previous full opera, *Peter Grimes*, it is like hearing Gluck after Lully: *Grimes* is episodic, sectional, and above all lyrical; *Billy Budd* is symphonic. Its continuity is manifest in the two-act form.* *Billy Budd* can be more fruitfully compared with its successor, *Gloriana*; *Billy Budd* deals with the image of a state, *Gloriana* with the reality. *Gloriana* has an almost baffling diffuseness; *Billy Budd* a claustrophobic condensing of mood and material. (There is virtually no recitative: even the conversation has memorable thematic structure, and the odd spoken words have the effect of unpitched percussion in a highly integrated texture.) We never for a moment forget the physical confinement of the ship, the rigid hierarchy of the Service, the continuous activity which is required simply to keep going, and the underlying tension of possible clashes with the enemy. These facts have their effect on the music—the "activities" of the ship create their own material, and maintaining the hierarchy is the backbone of the characterisation.

The most interesting structural feature is the main character, Captain Vere. Forster and Crozier created, in the Prologue and Epilogue, the situation of the old man looking

* As the most recent performance, December 1966, was taken in two acts, I shall discuss it in this version, as being the currently definitive one. The important advantage of this version is the continuity between Acts III and IV of the earlier performances. I have not undertaken to discuss different versions and editions of the operas in this book, since it is primarily addressed to audiences rather than historians—and, in any case, during the composer's lifetime, each new production is potentially a new edition: *vide pace* Handel!

back to the catastrophe—in Melville's novel this does not occur. But Melville himself began the novel when he was sixty-nine, twenty years after his previous book, and Eric Walter White* suggests that Vere looking back to "that far-away summer of 1797" is in part a portrayal of Melville, looking back to 1842, when his cousin was involved in a comparable incident in the American Navy. Melville's book is an attempt to justify the execution of three supposed mutineers, and the opera becomes Vere's attempt to justify his own handling of these incidents. Structurally the Prologue is in any case necessary to install Vere as the chief character: without it, Billy might contest the heroic role. Dramatically, Vere's importance lies in the fact that he is the only character in the opera with which an audience likely to be watching can identify. He has a duel role—in the action and outside it: a protagonist and a structural prop.

The themes of the opera offer a contrast to the confined physical scene; they could hardly be more comprehensive: good and evil in continual conflict on all levels of action (there is a very politically balanced view of this working throughout the hierarchy) and the imperfection of human justice. The librettists take pains to show Vere (as William Plomer later shows Gloriana) as a far from god-like ruler; he is a passionate, impetuous character whose inability to step outside the "enlightened" humanism of his age brings about the tragedy. The atmosphere is of violence and fear, obscured by the physical and metaphysical "cursed mist".

Musically the Prologue conveys both the conflict and the imperfection. Conflict is throughout the opera expressed in tonal ambivalence, bitonality; and the juxtaposition of notes, chords, and phrases a semitone apart. In this example it combines with the two descending fourths which form one of the few specific motifs in the opera, that are attached to Claggart, Master-at-Arms and the villain:

* In *Benjamin Britten, a sketch of his life and works.*

EX. 30

Vere attempts to depict himself: "I am an old man who has experienced much. I have been a man of action and have fought for my King and country at sea. I have also read books and studied, and pondered, and tried to fathom eternal truth. Much good has been shown me and much evil, and the good has never been perfect. There is always some flaw in it, some defect, some imperfection in the divine image . . . some stammer in the divine speech." It is a tranquil, reflective introduction which has not much to do with the impetuous character we are to see in the narrative of the opera. Vere becomes more impassioned, however, at this phrase:

EX. 31

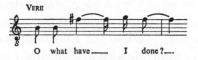

These notes, more flexible in application than a motif, represent the whole of the case for Vere's defence. They are used to suggest real or imagined, potential or actual mutiny. This phrase colours references to the Spithead and the Nore, two mutinies which informed the nightmares of most naval officers at this time; it appears as *The Rights o' Man*, innocently involved in the name of Billy's former ship, mistakenly seized upon as a reference to Thomas Paine's radical treatise; it appears when the Novice attempts to trap Billy into leading a mutiny and—most significant of all—it becomes the expansive melodic line of the men's working song, revealing the

raw material of mutiny—the cause and the justification, the
incipient threat.

The B♭ major/B minor ambivalence of the Prologue ends
with the opening of the first act—an incisive B minor. The
first scene is an extended portrayal of the normal and typical
activities on the *Indomitable*. The music is continuous; commands, shanties, conversations, soliloquies, choruses are in
turn imposed upon the continuous orchestral texture which
is in itself illustrative of the compression and congestion of life
at sea. An important rhythmic figure dominates the accom-

paniment to the stage action ♫ ♫♫♩ ♪ ♫ ♩. This, and

particularly the last group, is associated in the opera with
duty and the daily activity of running the ship. It is usually—
and in the first scene, which is particularly concerned with
establishing rank, exclusively—connected with non-commis-
sioned officers, though by the second act it has come to mean
all inflexible justice, from the King's Regulations to "the
laws of earth". Here it accompanies a holystoning operation
and is contrasted with the broadly lyrical working song of the
men, revealing a symphonic range of material as well as a
basis for the characterisation of large groups. These two ideas
are not interrupted till a new level of the hierarchy is introduced—the commissioned ranks have their own melodic vari-

ant of the ♫ ♩ pattern to the words "Life's not all play upon

a man of war". Their light-hearted lack of interest in the men
is pointed musically in the contrast between this and the "O
heave" chorus. A further recurrent motif is the Bosun's pipes
—flutes in seconds—used in connection with orders and
activities.

There is an incident at this point which stands out from
the continuity of the background action. The Bosun picks on
the Novice, almost without motivation, and sentences him to
twenty strokes of the cat. It is an incident which is both

typical and individual. The generalised atmosphere of violence is emphasised by the fact that such minor characters are involved—the Bosun, not Claggart; the nameless Novice, not Billy, Dankser, or Donald. However, it is a significant point in the plot. It is fear of a repetition of this punishment that drives the Novice to agree to tempt Billy in the next scene. The incident has also a purely musical value in that it gives rise to a sequel—the beautiful ensemble after the punishment, the only substantial point of repose in the whole scene.

It is dismissed as a typical, characteristic episode—"If anyone else wants the cat he can go slipping". After an intensified statement of "O heave", which is now used as an inarticulate protest at the cruelty that was normal, there is a complete change of mood: a prolonged preparation for a catalytic incident. The orchestra is dominated by woodwind and horn arpeggio figures—fanfares which seem to herald the return of the boarding party, but which in fact persist intermittently until Billy Budd's farewell to his former ship, *The Rights o' Man*; at which point the potential tragedy receives its impetus—the misleading interpretation, the unjustified accusation.

Before this, however, the boarding party returns with three impressed men. For the first time the music paints a sympathetic portrait of the officers, particularly in the Sailing Master's air, "We seem to have the devil's own luck". The view, carefully sustained in the opera, that problems of principle and behaviour existed for all ranks, is confirmed in this number which closely precedes the appearance of the Master-at-Arms. Every attempt is made on this occasion to show John Claggart as a man moulded by his superior officers. The *dolce* phrase, "Your honour, I am at your disposal", which he addresses to the first lieutenant is perhaps literally true and explains the contrasting *feroce* interrogation of the impressed men which he conducts. This point is underlined in his subsequent "I believe that is all you require, your honour"—

both phrases sung to the successive descending fourths shown
in Ex. 30.

There is a gradual speeding-up of the interviews, and
Billy's bursts-in with a new vitality, distinguished from his
fellow recruits not only by the faster tempo but by the wider
intervals—fifths instead of thirds—of his answers, which provoke responding fifths from the previously dispirited officers
—"it'll hearten us!" Billy's stammer contrasts with the fluent
style of his lyrical outbursts:

EX. 32

Most of his arias are developed from this style and most of the
accompaniments to them derive from the arpeggio fanfares of
this scene.

The officers are clearly delighted with Billy and uncomplicated in their reception of him. Claggart's reaction is more
conspicuous and considerably more ambiguous: over sonorous trombone and tuba chords he sings a phrase:

EX. 33

which occurs whenever he contemplates Billy's physical and
moral beauty. Later in this scene it is used at "Look after
your dress, take a pride in yourself, Beauty"; in the next
scene it becomes "Handsomely done, my lad, and handsome
is as handsome did it, too", and in the trial scene it is the
orchestral answer to the first lieutenant's question, "Why
should the Master-at-Arms accuse you wrongfully?" This
reaction is, then, the motive for Claggart's persecution of

Billy. It is a perversion, but not necessarily merely a sexual perversion. The themes of *Billy Budd* and much of the imagery raise the clash between Claggart and Billy to the status of a fight between Heaven and Hell: Billy "saves" and "blesses" Vere, he is "an angel of God", his is the "mystery of goodness"; Claggart "established an order such as reigns in hell", his world is "dark", he is "iniquity", Billy strikes him down calling him a "devil".

There is something very threatening in the strength and immediacy of Claggart's reaction, although it is at this stage apparently no other than complete approval. The deliberation of this passage is dispelled by Billy's exuberant aria "Billy Budd, King of the Birds", and the action, held up while Billy was being assessed, hurries on again—Billy sings farewell to his former ship using the phrase of Ex. 31 with the double result of aligning himself with the men and the pattern of their working song and of arousing the suspicions of the mutiny-haunted officers.

The first lieutenant consequently orders Claggart to "instruct [his] police" to keep a close watch on Billy. Even the initiative of doing this is denied Claggart. In the preceding scene with the impressed men and in the brief aria "Was I born yesterday?" Claggart is revealed as crushed between the officers and the seamen by the nature of his rank. He is also seen as the reverse side of Vere—Vere has "studied . . . and tried to fathom eternal truth", Claggart has also studied: "men and man's weakness" and "apprenticed [him] self to this hateful world". So in this aria the conflict between Claggart and Billy is already extended to include a duel between Vere and Claggart ("eternal truths" versus "this hateful world")—a deliberate widening of the issue which, I think, precludes a narrowly homosexual interpretation of Claggart's response to Billy. In the scene with Squeak, Claggart's mental as well as physical bullying is demonstrated. Billy's arpeggios return in the orchestra when Cleggart warns Squeak that he

will be "playing with fire". There is an ironic moment when
Claggart taunts: "He'll kill you if he catches you!" which—is
just what he does, except that it is Claggart whom Billy kills,
and without ever quite, comprehendingly, "catching" him.
This incident with Squeak is placed next to the following
scene, the Novice after his flogging, partly to suggest the
possibility of Claggart's later use of the Novice in place of
Squeak. The vocal casting is the clue: Claggart as a bass has
most of his scenes with tenors, invariably dominating them—
Red Whiskers, Squeak, and later the Novice. We are not,
then, surprised when he attempts to dominate Vere.

We earlier saw that the incident of the Novice's flogging
has both a general and a particular importance in the plot.
The same is true of its sequel. It is the first expression of
compassion in the opera, universalised by the chorus—"We're
all of us lost for ever on the endless sea"—yet intimately and
personally expressed by the Novice's friend ("I'll look after
you"), an utterly insignificant character, but here showing
an aspect of Vere's paternal role and ranging himself on the
side of the angels in this drama. Musically it is a marvellous
interlude. The saxophone melody, at first unaccompanied,
later underlaid by an undecorated inversion:

EX. 34

has an awareness of physical pain that is almost uncomfortable
to listen to; it expresses, too, the hopelessness of the comfort
offered to the Novice:

Novice's Friend: He's only a boy and he cannot walk!
Claggart: Let him crawl.

It is significant that the theme is itself both an outline of the minor sixth of the mutiny motif (here applied, as in "O heave", as a mutiny *motive*) and an inversion of "Starry Vere", the loyal acclamation we are shortly to hear uniting the officers and men.

One of the most moving lines in the ensemble is the Novice's Friend's interlocking minor thirds to which he sings "Come along, kid". This is transformed and extended in the ensuing *scherzando* episode into a new headlong phrase for the clarinet, the action hurrying on again. It is answered by a more hesitant bassoon phrase of successive and simultaneous major seconds. This twofold material continues in the orchestra against a comparatively light-hearted ensemble for Billy, Red Whiskers, Donald, and Dansker. And when this cluster of individual incidents is brought to a close in the scene finale, an assembly of the entire crew, the bassoon phrase is seen to be connected with the Bosun's pipes theme; the duty rhythm returns and, with a vast ternary feeling, the focus retreats, we take in the ship as a whole once more. And more than the ship: we are reminded of the war with France, which is the reason for most of the action of the plot—the harsh discipline, the press-ganging, the tension among the officers. It is also the reason for Vere's ultimate betrayal of Billy.

The second scene is a slowly-moving nocturne. In conspicuous contrast to the first scene there is a complete absence of any "activity" music. The atmosphere of relaxation extends over the whole ship. The mood of intimacy is sustained through each of the various episodes with each level of the hierarchy. The only tensions are that the ship is approaching enemy waters and Claggart's plot—often identified with the progress of the ship—is approaching execution.

After a beautiful and tranquil prelude, which includes a less than urgent reference to the duty rhythm, we are in Vere's cabin—this recalls the Prologue, and establishes a con-

tinuity between the character of Vere as exposed in the Prologue and the "man of action" acclaimed at the close of the
first scene. (It is interesting to contrast Vere with the Male
Chorus in *Lucretia*: both are immersed in classical history;
Vere, of the eighteenth century, aspiring to identify himself
with pre-Christian standards, "May their virtues be ours, and
their courage", while the Male Chorus, a first century-Chris-
tian, rejects their virtues and their courage. Vere's failure to
save Billy is a direct result of his classically slanted view of
life. He sees Billy as the consenting victim which expediency
and the good of his "people" require him to sacrifice.) The
material of the prelude recurs throughout this episode, a
genial scene between Vere and his officers with a fierce climax
when mutiny is mentioned—we have here an insight into the
horror with which these men regarded the possibility of
mutiny. Vere has a passionate aria of protest against the
mutiny at the Nore, the first of the impetuous outbursts which
are more characteristic of him in the course of the opera than
the reflective attitude in the Prologue and Epilogue. The
episodes of this nocturnal scene are more continuously lyrical
than in the first scene: the off-stage singing of shanties is
heard in Vere's cabin; it is interrupted by the duty rhythm,
loud and precise now, on trumpets, not in the relaxed
woodwind version of the prelude. The ship has reached enemy
waters and Vere dismisses his officers. As he returns to his
reading the shanties intrude again and are transferred to the
orchestra in a sensuously lyrical interlude—the men have,
throughout the opera, substantial melodic compensation for
the hardships of their life.

The shanties, like Vere's books, are the formal expression
of relaxation and escapism in his scene. As in the last episode,
there is a central violent climax, when Billy finds Squeak
(under Claggart's orders) tampering with his possessions.
Claggart interrupts the fight between them and punishes
Squeak not so much for failing to get the better of Billy but

D

rather as a relief to his own confused emotions—"the light shines in the darkness and the darkness comprehends it and suffers". Again the episodes overlap. There is a strong feeling of simultaneous action in this scene, in contrast to the first scene: a narration, a succession of incidents. Against a background of the third shanty of the scene, Claggart broods over his phrase "Handsomely done, my lad" (Ex. 33), which becomes, when the chorus dies away, his main aria.

This number, "O beauty, O handsomeness, goodness", goes some way—not all of the way—towards explaining the ambiguities in Claggart's character. It establishes (even allowing for the convention of the soliloquy) a morbid degree of introspection which contrasts with Vere, always an outward-looking character, so little given to brooding on the past that he has, in the Prologue, difficulty in recalling the events of this drama. Unlike Vere, Claggart knows himself. He is not a totally corrupt man, a Machiavel. The conflict is still going on, and in this aria he is in torment. There is a glimmer of unwillingness in the phrase "would that I had never encountered you!" and a perception of goodness when he sings, "if love still lives and grows strong where I cannot enter, what hope is there in my own dark world for me?" It is a sense of hopelessness that drives him to annihilate Billy and we feel that, in spite of the common cruelty and persecution of his environment, this is a unique decision for Claggart. The result is very beautiful musically. The mood alternates between Claggart's suffering in the presence of goodness (the Ex. 33 theme coloured as on all its appearances by the trombone which follows the voice line closely, at times coinciding with it, otherwise in canon—a slightly blurred image in the looking-glass), with a forceful middle section containing Claggart's resolve to destroy Billy. This part is built around rising scale passages of enormous energy. It is unusual for Claggart to have such a proportion of upward-moving phrases. Even his personal motif (see Ex. 30) is turned inside out and inverted

to the words "So may it be!" (Inversions of this phrase are
rare and always significant. Claggart uses it when he promises
Squeak "I'll make no trouble"—which would have been an
inversion of his normal behaviour had it turned out to be
true, and is, in fact, contradicted by his summary arrest of
Squeak after the fight with Billy. Vere uses the same shape
when he sings, "if I destroy goodness" and "it is for me to
destroy you", marking again the connection between himself
and Claggart and showing how he unwillingly carries out
Claggart's ironic predictions. At the end of this aria when
Claggart sings, "I will destroy you", we hear the straight
version of this motif, since what is horrifyingly abnormal for
Vere to contemplate is characteristic for Claggart.) The aria
finishes with another parallel between Claggart and Vere—
over sustained minor F chords (the key of the trial scene and
of Vere's aria "I accept their verdict") Claggart sings on one
note, "I, John Claggart, Master-at-Arms upon the *Indomitable*,
have you in my power", a passage exactly comparable with
"I, Edward Fairfax Vere, Captain of the *Indomitable*, lost with
all hands on the infinite sea"; the music here points a complex comparison between levels and efficacies of power.

Following immediately upon this aria, the Novice enters
to the pathetic saxophone melody of the flogging scene. This
episode, in which Claggart intimidates the Novice by violence
into betraying Billy, is perhaps the most moving in the opera.
The Novice is a more accessible character than Billy. It is
easier to sympathise with him and easier to understand his
reactions. We see him suffering in a way in which Billy is
never seen to suffer. In this despairing cry:

EX. 35

Yes, I'll work for you, I'll work for you, I've no choice.

he becomes (like Vere in the Prologue), if only momentarily, a character with whom the audience can identify themselves.

The nocturnal mood deepens as the next music portrays Billy asleep. This music is the same as that at the beginning of the last scene of the opera—a point which has no significance here, but which shows later how untroubled Billy's sleep then is: because of Vere's strengthening influence Billy is then as calm as he is now, before the tragic events begin. The Novice interrupts his sleep with a brisk, whispered incitement to mutiny—the mutiny motif is transformed into a crisp march as the Novice (very cleverly) puts Claggart's plan into action, and into a smoother muted-trumpet version when he offers him the gold as a bribe. The duet breaks up with Billy's stammer music when he realises the point to which the Novice's arguments have led.

The closing section of the act is between Billy and Dansker, establishing once again Billy's impenetrable goodness and his utter lack of suspicion in the face of Dansker's warnings. It is exuberant music which has thrown off all trace of the dreaming phrases, over a ground bass which is Claggart's motif and its inversion. Dansker's line moves with the bass, cynical, experienced, and unheeded. Billy himself has a filled-in version of the Claggart shape at the words "He [Claggart] calls me that sweet, pleasant fellow"—the sinister fourths transformed into a line of utter innocence.

The second act opens with a splendidly organised return to the activity music which was paramount in the first scene of the opera. Everything that happens in the opera has the two dramatic functions of general effect and particular contribution to the plot. Here the attempted sea-fight is part of the working background of the ship, as well as enacting the image of Vere pursuing his moral enemy through the mists of distrust.

The *vivace* prelude is based, like so much of the instru-

mental music in this opera, on two interposed ideas. The
woodwind and trumpets have a chordal figure:

Ex. 36

which is later identified with the chorus "This is our moment,
the moment we've been waiting for." It is linked with the
mutiny motif by being the interval of a fifth turning inwards
by a semitone, instead of outwards, an additional aspect of
the characterisation of the men. It is here answered by—and
later combined with—a timpani and strings rhythm, perhaps
representing the suspense of waiting for action, certainly
used to portray the frustration of failure at the close of the
episode. An important development of Ex. 36 is its arpeggio
shape extended upwards through different keys—this appears
at references to, and at the physical presence of the mist; it
results in a blurring and distortion of the fighting theme, and
the disappointment of the hopes that theme stands for.

Before the fight there is a brief scene between Vere and
Claggart. Claggart enters to an evil, urgent semitone shift:

Ex. 37

linked vitally to the musical argument not only by the
juxtaposition of keys and chords a semitone apart, which
usually prefaces Claggart's entries, but also because these
notes are another way of outlining the mutiny pattern,
particularly the transformation of it used when the Novice
tempted Billy with gold. This chord shift is combined with an
inversion of the mutiny motif (in the bass line) in Claggart's
tentative arioso, "With great regret do I disturb your

honour". He is interrupted before he reveals the content of his accusation. Back to the action, the Ex. 36 phrase is now answered by the duty rhythm: an enemy sail has been sighted, and "the mist is gone!"

The ensuing choral ensemble is based on a further variant of Ex. 36 which adds a major seventh to the rising arpeggio and descends by another chord. Then the mood of random excitement is banished and the organisation of a sea-fight is put into motion. The timpani plus strings rhythm from the act prelude becomes an *ostinato* accompaniment to a broad and purposeful version of Ex. 36, the chorus "This is our moment". Against these two continuing streams of music the Gunners, Seamen, After-Guardsmen, Powder Monkeys, and Marines are added in sequence to a large visual and aural build-up (like Noye's animals coming out of the Ark). Each section has its own melodic material which is finally combined and superimposed on the "This is our moment" chorus and the recurrent rhythm. All this tremendous potential action now—literally—hangs fire, waiting for Vere's command. They are out of range, and in an exquisite quiet climax the chorus conjure up the wind with a hymn that must have taken Vere back to Aulis! It is a moment of great tension: the *pianissimo* chorus, with single phrases relating to the anxious progress of the ship being passed along the hierarchical lines of communication. It is Vere who releases the tension and orders them to try a shot. Immediately the suspense has vanished and with a short, loud, unaccompanied climax the shot is fired. It falls short and the waiting tension begins again, to be released this time by the return of the mist. The men disperse to a subdued diminished-chord version of their chorus, now singing "Gone is our moment . . ."

The act prelude is recapitulated with diminished dynamics, and Britten reworks the drama from the point of view of Claggart, Vere, and Billy. This is Claggart's moment, the moment he has been waiting for. With the chord shift of Ex.

37 he takes up the arioso which was interrupted before the fight preparations. Claggart is either completely insensitive to Vere's cool and discouraging reception of him—like a plodding subordinate who must make the whole of the speech he has prepared—or, more consistent with the portrait that has been built up, he enjoys the same power over Vere (who must in reason listen to the reports of his "police") as he wields over the miserable Squeak and Novice. At all events, he holds Vere's unwilling attention with a description of an unnamed mutineer (the accompaniment expresses the mutiny figure in linear, chordal, and superimposed transformations), saving the vital word, "mutiny", for a whispered phrase, as Vere did to his officers in the second scene of Act I. There, for Vere, it was "a word which we scarcely dare speak"; now he takes it up *forte*—"mutiny? I'm not to be scared by words!"— with the inconsistency of a passionate man. Claggart describes the tempting of Billy, by the Novice, reversing the roles. The accompaniment continues to evolve from the mutiny phrase in a pattern which is really derived from Ex. 37, opened out to be reminiscent of the Novice's temptation scene in the first act. This shape recurs when Claggart accuses Billy of bribery in the next scene.

Vere immediately puts his finger on the weak point in the scheme—"How came the boy by gold, a common seaman? Strange story!" When Claggart names Billy as the mutineer, Vere launches into a spontaneous defence of him: "Nay, you're mistaken. Your police have deceived you. Don't come to me with so foggy a tale." He is driven by Claggart's continued accusations into forcing a confrontation between Claggart and Billy. And with Vere's reminder—"There's a yard-arm for a false witness"—the struggle is a life and death one for both. Vere precipitates the tragedy at this point because he cannot bear any uncertainty about Billy's character, not because of his fear of mutiny. Billy's influence over Vere is seen in this number, which recalls the fluent lyricism of Billy's aria style rather than the agitated leaping intervals of Vere's aria denouncing the mutiny at the Nore. The pounding rhythm in the orchestra continues through the conversation arranging the interview with Billy, and Claggart's opportunity to accuse him. It stops only with the reappearance of the mist motif, which introduces an ironic episode in which Vere damns the "confusion without and within" while his officers bemoan the physical mist and the loss of the French ship.

In a phrase which first appeared in the scene in his cabin in Act I, Vere prays for "the light of clear Heaven to separate evil from good". This phrase becomes, in an orchestral interlude, a kind of chorale on the brass against an extension and development of the mist theme, presumably representing the doubts and aspirations in Vere's mind. Towards the end of the interlude the music turns to a radiant D major; Billy's characteristic fanfares flood the orchestra and continue through much of the next scene. In his cabin, Vere is now confident that "the boy whom [Claggart] would destroy . . . is good". He undergoes several changes of opinion about this in the ensuing minutes, but at this point "the mists are vanishing" and he is determined to confound Claggart and the evil he represents. Billy enters—the arpeggios continue in a new horn version—and, misled into expecting his promotion, he protests his loyalty to Vere: "I'd die for you". The "duty" rhythmic pattern announces Claggart's arrival and he enters to an apparently new theme which is simply a devious variant of the mutiny motif again, now transformed into the accusation theme. It entwines in canon when Claggart enters. It is contrasted with a sharp, clear return to D major and the duty rhythm when Vere addresses the "accuser and accused"; it returns to colour Vere's reference to "the penalties of falsehood". This theme becomes, naturally, Claggart's vocal line when he formally accuses Billy. Vere orders Billy, to the duty motif, to answer the accusations. Billy replies only with his

stammer, overcome by his outraged reaction. It seems to be
Vere's kindly gesture, in aligning himself with Billy as closely
as he dares, that releases the physical force of anger in Billy.
And Billy strikes Claggart dead. The orchestra has a vivid
portrayal of the literal disintegration of Claggart's being
through the fragmentation of his motif down the orchestra.

Vere then behaves quite extraordinarily. Without making
any attempt to communicate with him or understand his
behaviour, he sends Billy to wait in the adjacent stateroom
and immediately summons his officers.* The absence of any
attempt on Vere's part to come to terms with the situation
alone is a most striking contrast between his character and
Claggart's. The lack of a real intimacy between Vere and his
officers emerged from the nocturnal scene in the first act—
Vere does not even speak the same language. Yet at this
highly personal dilemma he hurries to share the situation with
them, realising only after he has sent the message that he now
sees "all the mists concealed", and that consequently it is not
Billy's trial but his. The Claggart/Vere conflict has now
replaced the Claggart/Billy antithesis, even though Claggart
is now dead. It is pointed musically with utter simplicity in
the phrase "It is I whom the Devil awaits": Claggart's motif
inverted for the first half of the phrase (Vere) and in situ for
the word "Devil".

The conduct of the trial is further evidence of Vere's
extreme agitation. He announces baldly and misleadingly to
the officers, "Gentlemen, William Budd here has killed the
Master-at-Arms", while simultaneously acknowledging in an

---

* In Melville's novel the extraordinary nature of Vere's total behaviour
is discussed at length, but at this particular point in the story he is given
a little time to breathe: after confirming that Claggart was dead, "Vere
with one hand covering his face stood to all appearance as impassive as
the object at his feet. Was he absorbed in taking all the bearings of the
event and what was best not only now at once to be done, but also in the
sequel? Slowly he uncovered his face; and the effect was as if the moon
emerging from eclipse should reappear with quite another aspect than
that which had gone into hiding . . ."

aside that Claggart was "struck by an angel, an angel of God, yet the angel must hang". This line is a continuation of Vere's soliloquy before the officers arrived, dealing with his own moral trial which he knows to be taking place. The answering trio of the two lieutenants and the Sailing Master and the subsequent ensembles for these officers are splendidly true and effective, from their individualised first reactions to an increasing degree of agreement and their final unanimity when they reach their verdict. The duty motif, predictably, spurs Vere on to summoning the "drumhead court". The fact that this is *his* trial is portrayed (in a way reminiscent of the Prologue of *Peter Grimes*) when he appears as witness, to be cross-examined by his own officers. An instrumental preface to the trial sets in apposition the accusation motif and the Ex. 33 phrase, stating as unambiguously as if it were verbal that all Claggart could accuse Billy of was "beauty, hand-someness, goodness". This point is made again in the trial— the first lieutenant asks Billy, "Why should the Master-at-Arms accuse you wrongfully?" The orchestra replies repeatedly and explicitly when Billy cannot and Vere will not do so. When the first lieutenant asks Billy if he has anything more to say, Billy appeals to Vere—"Captain Vere, save me! I'd have died for you", and the horn recalls the exultant texture of Billy's avowal of this, before the tragedy—at a time, moreover, when Vere was confidently on Billy's side, which must make an agonising contrast for him here.

Billy is sent out while the orchestra inverts the extended accusation theme which opened the trial. In the following ensemble the three officers try the problem from all points of view and come to the fateful conclusion that:

EX. 38

1ST LIEUTENANT
SAILING MASTER
LIEUTENANT RATCLIFFE

We've no   choice.

These notes, like the dilemma, they try all ways round. In a
tense passage we hear the rival appeals of the officers—"Sir,
help us with your knowledge and wisdom . . . grant us your
guidance"—and the *pianissimo* (interior) promptings of the
duty rhythm on muted trumpets. To this rhythm Vere accepts
their verdict of hanging and the scene with the *ritornello* of the
accusation and beauty-handsomeness-goodness motifs whispered on the harp.

As in *Lucretia*, there are three funeral marches around the
protagonist's death. The first is Vere's next aria, "I accept
their verdict". It is punctuated throughout with the duty
motif on the trumpets, now unmuted, which here represents
the limitations of human justice. Vere reveals that he has also
accepted a verdict against himself, though he is fully aware of
the short-lived logic and even splendour of his decision:

EX. 39

This expansive thought is soon dwarfed in the face of the
"divine judgement of Heaven" and he is "cooped in this
narrow cabin". The horn, which reminded Vere in the trial
of his betrayal of Billy's absolute trust in him, now hounds
him into a state of panic—"Before what tribunal do I stand
if I destroy goodness? . . . I, Edward Fairfax Vere, Captain
of the *Indomitable*, lost with all hands on the infinite sea." In a
coda, his thoughts turn to Billy, while the orchestra has a fast
and passionate version of the saxophone melody of Ex. 34. It
effects—if it is recognised—a return to a consideration of

punishment and suffering here and now: "I am the messenger of death. How can he pardon? How receive me?" The answer is given once more in musical rather than verbal terms. Vere goes into the cabin where Billy is waiting, leaving the orchestra to play a series of chords, each coloured with a separate section of instruments and dynamic intensity, expressing by sonority alone the extremely complex range of reactions and emotions taking place behind the closed door.

This extended cadence resolves with the opening of the next scene—it is nearly morning and Billy is half asleep, dreaming to the sleepy music we heard in the previous act when the Novice woke him and tempted him. The constant tonic, indeed the costant F major pedal chord, is very striking after the spectrum of chord colour at the end of the previous scene. This is the first moment of emotional repose since Vere's confident perception of good and evil in his cabin before Claggart's accusation ("Claggart, John Claggart, beware! I'm not so easily deceived"). It is, of course, all the more amazing that this calm emanates from a man in irons who is shortly to be executed; but that is Billy's "mystery of goodness", the consenting sacrifice which can "save" Vere. In spite of this, Billy is not at all withdrawn. With Dansker we are reminded that he is very much one of the men, although he has been flung into the lives of Vere and his officers. Because of the musical organisation of the opera, Dansker is able to suggest in five notes ("They swear you shan't swing") the mutiny threatened and, although Billy rejects it, this possibility is an extra tension during the last scene of the opera. The beginning of Billy's dreaming aria was essentially a continuation of the overtly sexual cadential chords of the preceding scene: at the end of this episode they return (inexactly), gradually intruding on Billy's ecstatic "And farewell to ye, old *Rights o' Man*", conspicuously at the words "I'm contented", and taking over the entire accompaniment when he sings: "I'm strong, and I know it, and I'll stay strong . . .

and that's all . . . that's enough." An orchestral interlude
reviews the dramatic situation, alternating at first phrases
of Billy-characterising arpeggio fanfares with the theme
attached to the verdict, "Hanging from the yard-arm" (given
a new counter-subject), and later the verdict theme with
the duty motif and the Bosun's pipes.

We now come to the second funeral march. In the early-
morning light the entire crew silently assembles in the same
order and to the same melodic tags that formed the basis of
their preparations for the fight at the beginning of the act.
Vere enters to the "Starry Vere" motif and another group of
the chords, harking back to the unforgettable close of the
verdict scene. Billy is heralded by his own fanfares, interrupted by the "hanging" phrase. The first lieutenant reads
the sentence. Billy suddenly sings, "Starry Vere, God bless
you!" which is taken up immediately by the entire assembly.
Billy's death is dealt with instrumentally—a long rising scale
as he ascends the mast and the "hanging" phrase which is now
sufficiently verbalised to be explanatory. The fulfilment of
dramatic situations in purely musical terms is a satisfying
feature of *Billy Budd*. The musical and textural treatment of
the mutiny motif throughout the opera gives an overwhelm-
ing significance to the worldless chorus which now starts up—
mutiny which we have only seen discussed, simulated, and
threatened till now, mutiny for which we have seen ample
cause, held in check only by even more dangerous provoca-
tion. To avert the possibility of mutiny, Vere sacrifices Billy,
and in doing so comes nearer to arousing one than at any
previous point in the opera. When the rebellious chorus turns
into "O heave" as it is overcome, we are very aware of a
continuing explosive situation, kept underground but not
extinguished by the habitually inflexible "laws of earth".

The scene merges into Vere's Epilogue, which begins like
the Prologue, but soon adds a recurrent timpani figure,
transforming it into the third funeral march. The narration

of Billy's death gives way to wider considerations: "I could
have saved him. He knew it, even his shipmates knew it,
though earthly laws silenced them", and the Bosun's pipes
and the duty rhythm show how they were silenced. Vere
asks, as in the Prologue, "O what have I done?" and at this
stage in the work we can recognise the orchestral answer—
duty. Instead of the "confusion, so much is confusion!"
passage in the Prologue, we have a transformation of Billy's
last aria, "And farewell to ye, old *Rights o' Man*"—a more
tranquil, Vere-of-the-Epilogue characterised version, but
underlining the fact that his peace of mind is bequeathed
him by Billy. The chords from the verdict scene are incorporated in the orchestral texture which retains the rocking
intervals of the "infinite sea" now settled increasingly
firmly in B♭ major. The confidence expressed in the tonality
is reflected in the wide, untroubled intervals to which the
words "I am an old man now . . ." are set, in contrast to the
Prologue. The Epilogue, itself a recession from the drama,
now recedes further, dynamically dropping away from a big
climax, and dropping vocally in pitch to an unaccompanied
finish. The position of Vere as audience-representative in the
opera is sealed for me in the tremendous withdrawal in the
words here—"and my mind can go back in peace to that far-
away Summer of seventeen hundred and ninety seven, long
ago now, years ago, *centuries ago* . . ."

Chapter six

Gloriana

Libretto by William Plomer.
First performed at Covent Garden, June 1953.

CHARACTERS

QUEEN ELIZABETH I — Joan Cross, *soprano*
ROBERT DEVEREUX, Earl of Essex — Peter Pears, *tenor*
FRANCES, Countess of Essex — Monica Sinclair, *mezzo-soprano*

CHARLES BLOUNT, Lord Mountjoy — Geraint Evans, *baritone*
PENELOPE, Lady Rich, sister to Essex — Jennifer Vyvyan, *soprano*
SIR ROBERT CECIL, secretary of the Council — Arnold Matters, *baritone*
SIR WALTER RALEIGH, captain of the Guard — Frederick Dalberg, *bass*
HENRY CUFFE, a satellite of Essex — Ronald Lewis, *baritone*
A LADY-IN-WAITING — Adele Leigh, *soprano*
A BLIND BALLAD-SINGER — Inia Te Wiata, *bass*
THE RECORDER OF NORWICH — Michael Langdon, *bass*
A HOUSEWIFE — Edith Coates, *mezzo-soprano*

THE SPIRIT OF THE MASQUE — William McAlpine, *tenor*
THE MASTER OF CEREMONIES — David Tree, *tenor*
THE CITY CRIER — Rhydderch Davies, *baritone*

CHORUS; DANCERS; ACTORS; MUSICIANS
Conductor: John Pritchard
Producer: Basil Coleman
Designer: John Piper
Choreographer: John Cranko
Chorus Master: Douglas Robinson

ACT I, SCENE I : The story takes place in England in the later years of Queen Elizabeth I's reign, which lasted from 1558 to 1603. Outside a tilting-ground, during a tournament. The Earl of Essex, learning of Mountjoy's prowess in the tournament, incites him to a duel which the entry of Queen Elizabeth interrupts; Gloriana orders the two lords to forget their quarrel and "come to court . . . together".

SCENE 2: In her private apartment at Nonesuch, Elizabeth conducts politics with Cecil and more private business with Essex. Essex sings two lute songs to divert her, protests his love, and asks to be sent to Ireland to quell the rebel Tyrone. The Queen dismisses him and rededicates herself to her duty and her people.

ACT II, SCENE I : The Guildhall at Norwich. On progress through the city, the Queen is entertained by a rustic masque.

SCENE 2: At night in the garden of Essex House in the Strand. Mountjoy and Penelope Rich (Essex's sister) have a romantic assignation which is disturbed by the entry of Essex, complaining to his wife that the Queen will not give him the advancement he craves. Lady Essex attempts to restrain her husband's ambition, but Mountjoy and Penelope join with Essex in conspiring to seize power.

SCENE 3: Dancing at the Palace of Whitehall at night. Lady Essex arrives in a particularly splendid dress. Elizabeth is piqued, and to show her disapproval arranges to have the dress stolen; she appears in it herself—it is too short for the

Queen and the effect is ridiculous. When she retires for a second time the conspirators of the previous scene comfort Lady Essex, while Essex becomes increasingly bitter against the Queen. At the height of his outburst Elizabeth returns and announces the appointment of Essex as Lord Deputy in Ireland.

ACT III, SCENE I: An ante-room to the Queen's dressing-room at Nonesuch. Essex has returned to England un-announced and breaks in upon the Queen before she is dressed, painted, or bewigged. Essex is confused and the Queen is kind, but he cannot rekindle the intimacies of the first Act; and when she dismisses him, Elizabeth directs Cecil to have Essex placed under guard—she has "failed to tame [her] thoroughbred".

SCENE 2: A street in the City of London. Essex, with a hand-ful of supporters, breaks out and attempts to "rouse up all the city". He fails disastrously and is proclaimed a traitor.

SCENE 3: A room in the Palace of Whitehall. Essex has been found guilty and condemned to die. The Queen has yet to sign the death-warrant. She is petitioned by Lady Essex and Penelope Rich. Lady Essex pleads for her children and the Queen promises to protect them; she is gracious and kind. Penelope's arrogant manner antagonises her, however, and in her anger Elizabeth quickly signs the death-warrant.

EPILOGUE: The stage darkens and the Queen is left alone. Time and place become fluid, as various scenes from the last years of Elizabeth's life are enacted in spoken dialogue against the second lute song in the orchestra. Gloriana dies to the strains of both the private love and the public homage she lived to inspire.

"The first performance of *Gloriana* took place on the 8th of July 1953, at the Royal Opera House, Covent Garden, in the presence of Her Majesty the Queen."

"This work is dedicated by gracious permission to Her Majesty Queen Elizabeth II in honour of whose Coronation it was composed."

Contrary to all appearances *Gloriana* was not merely an occasional opera. It is by virtue of its interior nature the antithesis of a one-occasion work. Its subject is so vast, and the treatment so diffuse, that it can only be grasped as a whole after the event—or preferably on a second exposure to it. Britten had not previously written an opera that was not in some way concerned with limiting factors, from the physical limitations of a chamber orchestra, children's or all-male voices, to the psychological limitations of the nineteenth-century provincial collective mentality. In *Gloriana* all of these are swept away. It is set in an age which—certainly in 1953—was felt to be peculiarly relevant to inspire our own times; an age, moreover, whose musical language is better known to us than that of any intervening period. And it deals not with a borough, but a nation. On this point—the opera's sheer vastness and scope—depend its successes and its failures.

The book, Lytton Strachey's *Elizabeth and Essex*, on which the libretto is avowedly based is a red herring. The opera is not an account of the relationship of Elizabeth and Essex. Essex is far too patchily drawn and the proportions are quite wrong for this to be so. In fact, Essex is consciously withdrawn from prominence of a number of occasions. He is the most representative of Elizabeth's decorative but ineffectual favourites, but Mountjoy is early shown to enjoy nearly similar intimacies, and Raleigh, equal power. The "love" between Elizabeth and Essex was of Elizabeth's creating: "as her charms grew less, her insistence on their presence grew greater. She had been content with the devoted homage of her contemporaries; but from the young men who surrounded her in her old age she required—and received—the expressions of romantic passion . . ." (Strachey). The opera has a triple theme: it is about kingship—the relationship between a sovereign and her people; it also contains an intimate portrait of the public and private person of the Queen; and it is a portrayal—necessarily brief but very varied—of the age.

Musically, this last point creates problems. To revivify the richest previous age in our musical history, the language of the opera must take some cognisance of the language of the period, without falling into worthless pastiche. In *Gloriana* we become aware of the musical style the originals of the characters knew. At times it is nearer the surface than others. And its spirit does imbue the opera in some very concrete ways: there is, of course, the deliberate rethinking of madrigals and court dances in the second act, but there is also the harmonic fingerprint of the opera—common chords on neighbouring degrees of the scale—that gives a bright clarity to the "public" scenes, and this sort of directness to the "private" ones:

EX. 40

And change of ho - ly thoughts to make him mer - ry.

The first scene is a taste of public life. It opens with an
orchestral prelude which exactly anticipates the action and
the music of the beginning of the scene. It is a jousting
tournament, and in the prelude we hear the sennets and the
charges in a series of variations on the theme of the first
fanfare:

EX. 41

All this is repeated when the curtain rises: the fanfares
become the off-stage crowd, following the fortunes of their
favourite, Mountjoy, in the lists; the quicker music accompanies Cuffe's description of the action and Essex's reactions.
Almost at once Essex reveals his jealousy in a phrase which
appeared as a counter-subject in the prelude: to the words
"I hate the name of him" he sings notes which later condemn
him ("Essex is guilty" in the last act). The only other important theme in this movement is the inconspicuous appearance of the "homage" chorus which we are soon to hear sung
off-stage.

It is an awkward beginning for the opera. Dramatically, it
is concerned with a side-issue: although Essex's jealousy was a

pertinent factor in his historical career (and this is one of the many scenes in the opera which is based on a historical incident) it is not of tremendous importance in this opera. And the fact that this particular jealousy—of Mountjoy—is about to be negated by a lifelong (or at least opera-long) friendship makes it a less than significant incident. The importance of this sort of occurrence for the Queen is revealed in passing at the end of the next scene: "on rivalries 'tis safe for kings to base their power". It has more significance—and attraction—for her than for the audience.

The opera starts dramatically with the first choral appearance (still off-stage) of the hymn of homage:

EX. 42

This returning chorus expresses the nation's devotion to its Queen, an operatic as well as historical point. Mountjoy enters singing the same notes, identifying himself with the attitude Elizabeth required of her favourites and binding himself—visually—to the royal favour in the form of a gold chess piece. Essex, out to pick a quarrel, immediately turns the music away from the homage chorus and the "public" key of D major into D minor, the key of his petulance towards the Queen. One phrase—the D-minor arpeggio at "a favour

now for every fool"—is to be associated in an ambiguous way
with his standing in the Queen's favour; it is the phrase in
which he is appointed "Lord Deputy in Ireland"—an
appointment which was, indeed, according to Strachey, a
favour for a fool. But this phrase is also, in a major key and
with an altered ending, the moving consolation he offers his
wife in the dress incident—"Good Frances, do not weep";
and again in this version, the proud, miscalculated petition for
mercy his sister sings in the last act—"The noble Earl of
Essex Was born to fame and fortune . . ."

In the middle of the duel the Queen arrives. Whenever she
is on stage the dramatic inconsistencies are unimportant. For
this formidable portrait, Britten does not confine her music
inside a handful of motifs. It is a very wide-ranging style;
usually noble, often declamatory, rarely lyrical. It is a style
which—embracing all forms of communication from the
spoken word to the passionate duets with Essex—only gradually emerges as personal or indeed even consistent. Like the
opera itself, it has a physical range which is difficult to assess
and appreciate at any one moment in the work.

Everything in the opera is made subservient to the projection of Elizabeth's character. This scene is interspersed
with short choral phrases, describing, not contributing to, the
action; they serve as a reminder that this is a court scene, not
a private one—a vital distinction in this opera. There is a
brief, memorable duet for Essex and Mountjoy, subtitled in
the score "The Two Lords' Explanation": all the scenes are
divided into incidents in this way, emphasising the episodic
construction of the scenes and, indeed, of the entire opera.
The minor characters—Raleigh and Cecil in particular—
exist musically almost wholly in a series of closed forms, not
so much arias as songs: there is no character development.
They are presented as ready-made historical figures. Raleigh,
in his song "The bluefly and the bee", emerges as the character of the scene. As with Cecil, we need background knowledge

of the part he played in Essex's downfall, to understand his full significance.

Mutual dislike of Raleigh draws Essex and Mountjoy together. There follows an "Ensemble of Reconciliation", a movement with a curiously mechanical texture—curious until we recall the "divisions" of keyboard music of the age, the pattern of which this imitates. It culminates in another appearance of the homage chorus and the Queen departs to the accompaniment of similar on-stage trumpet fanfares to those which heralded her arrival.

Scene 2 is in great contrast. It is a private scene: the Queen closeted with her wise councillor (Cecil) and her un-wise pseudo-lover (Essex). It is easy to misread the opera's intentions in this scene, and to expect to find a plot develop-ing. There is no plot—other than the themes mentioned pre-viously—and the purpose of the scene is to show the Queen in *typical* incidents and relationships. The Prelude recalls both the fight between Essex and Mountjoy and the "Essex favour" arpeggios. The Queen reveals these topics to be the subjects of her thoughts. Cecil—to whom she reveals them—is an interesting figure in the drama; the hunchback secretary Elizabeth trusted in preference to her merely decorative young men. His "Song of Government" is apt historically and a miracle of onomatopoeia musically, with a creeping "twos against threes" accompaniment which can only be described as shifty, and a vocal line that is busy without getting any-where. Before this, the Queen sang a "Queen-ship" song over a repeated six-note accompanying figure

EX. 43

This figure is now distorted

EX. 44

when Cecil introduces "cares of state" to the Queen's attention. The opera assumes that the audience will know that the
situation with Spain was a typical—if not perpetual—"care"
for the Queen, rather than an incident to be developed. When
Essex enters, and Cecil leaves, the "cares of state" motif still
dominates the accompaniment. The Earl's first, gay lute song
cannot dislodge it.

The second lute song, which will surely always be the most
famous number in the opera, is a detached as well as detach-
able piece; unlike Raleigh's and Cecil's songs, but like the
first lute song, it is isolated from the conversation level of the
drama in being a conscious art song. Nevertheless its context
gives it added meanings—it is the Queen's escape from "cares
of state" and it is also her romantic dream: "spirit us *both*
away". It acquires a further richness when we know it to be
written by the historical Earl of Essex—this historical realism
also applies to many of the Queen's speeches. But a poem is
more in touch with the personality of the writer than either
public speech or reported conversation. (Yet we cannot but
agree with Elizabeth when she declares: " 'tis a conceit, it is
not you"; Essex had numerous opportunities to "retire" when
troubles at court became dangerous, but he could not live
without both royal and popular esteem. In the most brilliant
sentence of his book, Strachey wrote, of Francis Bacon, "it is
almost always disastrous not to be a poet"—disaster certainly
overwhelmed Essex when he ceased to be one.) The style of
the whole opera runs a risk—the risk of coming too near to
pastiche in casting a twentieth-century eye over the musical

language of an earlier period. The risk is justified when this intensely lovely song is a result. It is set in a dark C minor which effectively withdraws it from the bright keys of public life even for anyone as insensitive in general to actual keys as the average audience and the author. In disjointed phrases the music illuminates the conventional erotic imagery with a radiance which might well have warmed Elizabeth:

EX. 45

The opera moves from one melodic joy to another—Elizabeth and Essex have an enchanting duet ("O heretofore Though ringed with foes . . ."). That this is all an escapist's dream is emphasised when the Queen dismisses Essex with the "cares of state" motif. Elizabeth invokes her relationship with her people—who materialises in a quotation of the homage theme on the trombones—to negate Essex's influence. The musical style of her characterisation is extended by this prayer —first recited, then delivered in a tense, limited, plainsong-like theme. Already in the first act we are involved in a vast canvas.

The second act is the most obviously balanced of the three:
two contrasted public scenes enclosing an intimate one;
daylight, moonlight, candlelight. In the outer scenes we find
a kind portrait of the Queen, an unkind one and a puzzling
one; homage offered to her and honours bestowed by her.
After the public and private language of the first act we are
now introduced to provincial speech. It would have been an
incomplete picture of the age without some reference to the
immensely stage-worthy entertainments offered to the Queen
on progress.*

In the preceding scene, descending perfect fourths were
associated with royal duty, descending and augmented with
royal cares. The prelude to this scene, and the "hurrahs!" of
the people of Norwich, bristle with ascending perfect fourths
which can be identified with royal recreation. The incident
with the elderly Recorder shows the Queen at her most
benign, indulging in the love-affair with a nation which was
her ideal of monachy. Essex is jealous as well as bored. And
Cecil rebukes him, refering to the homage theme, "to be on
progress with her Majesty, is that no honour to you now?"

The masque is a splendid reinterpretation of madrigal
style. Sheer delight at the fresh melodic lines and rhythmic
variety again dismisses any thoughts of pastiche. It is also a
kind of relaxation to have a completed episode: the scenes
and incidents in the first act were all fragments; without some

* E. S. Turner, in *The Court of St James's*, gives this account of a Norwich
visit: "At Norwich the mayor addressed the Queen in Latin. This time
she did not feel it incumbent on her to reply in the same tongue. Bad
weather preserved her from a speech by "King Gurgunt, sometime King
of England", but Commonwealth treated her to a rhymed disquisition
on weaving. Norwich also devised a charade in which Chastity set about
Cupid and turned him out of his coach, then came up to congratulate
the Queen on retaining her virginity. In the background Wantonness and
Riot flitted enviously. Chastity's maids-in-waiting, Modesty, Temper-
ance, Good Exercise and Shamefastness, then sang a ditty to prove that
"chaste life for loss of pleasures short doth win immortal praise", and
that "chaste life hath merry moods and soundly taketh rest", and "lewd
life cuts off his days". A bevy of nymphs were scheduled to pop out of
caves to greet the Queen, but rain stopped play."

historical knowledge on the part of the audience they could seem unsatisfying rather than meaningful. The masque satisfies the desire for spectacle, which was frustrated by the off-stage tournament, and the desire for a self-sufficient episode which neither the Cecil interview nor the Essex situation meet.

The masque is, however, patently unreal; the jousting, a replica of warfare; Essex's devotion, a mirage projected by the Queen's own mind. The opera has so far been an artifice, the illusion of reality sustained by the smooth working of the puppets. From this point in the opera, Act II, Scene 2, three characters emerge who act entirely spontaneously: Mountjoy (in many ways a new man since his reconciliation with Essex in the first scene of Act I), Penelope Rich, Essex's sister (the "Stella" of Sir Philip Sidney's sonnets), and Lady Essex— the only wholly sympathetic character in the opera. The absence of Gloriana and her court makes for a ravishing change of tone colour in this moonlit garden scene—flutes, celesta, and pizzicato muted strings. Mountjoy and Penelope, for whom this is an assignation, have a tender, lyrical scene which seems, however, pale, restrained and unimpassioned after the exposition of a love between a people and their sovereign. Essex and Lady Essex enter, unaware of the lovers. A clarinet and bass clarinet change the colour to the thicker, darker tone of Essex's ambition. (Clarinets accompany the "Lord Deputy in Ireland" appointment; they are also conspicuous when he returns from Ireland, when the Ballad Singer foretells the "dreadful danger" of his rebellion; and when Lady Essex, Penelope, and Mountjoy plead for him in tha last act.) His present music strides in impatient dotted minor ninths—

ESSEX: Whatever step I take the Queen will bar my way.
LADY ESSEX: The Queen knows your valour!
ESSEX: She knoweth not how quick my patience ebbs.

LADY ESSEX: A subject must obey.
ESSEX: Caprice, rebuff, delay . . .

The couples meet and, impotently restrained by Lady Essex, plot treasonably "ourselves to rule the land". Essex was a potential traitor almost by virtue of his rank: "the spirit of ancient feudalism was not quite exhausted. Once more before the reign was over, it flamed up, embodied in a single individual—Robert Devereux, Earl of Essex. The flame was glorious—radiant with the colours of antique knighthood and the flashing gallantries of the past; but no substance fed it; flaring wildly, it tossed to and fro in the wind; it was suddenly put out." Essex was, in fact, too weak a character to be a serious threat to the throne even in his final abortive attempt chronicled in the last act. Mountjoy was a more worldly figure, plotting with Essex when success seemed possible, refusing to carry out their wilder schemes when failure became apparent. Penelope is a splendidly drawn character as far as the opera is concerned: the family failing of excessive pride turns to a shrewish but thoughtless eagerness to spur on her men to disaster.

Act II, Scene 3, is in several ways the apparent counterpart of Scene 1: the court at home, after the court on progress; the "town" dances after the rustic masque; the "real" music (performed on stage) of these dances, compared with "real" madrigals. All seems set for another scene the function of which is pageantry and colour. But it has a surprising result. Through the medium of the "public" style of this scene and undistracted by the resplendent visual element emerges a more revealing portrait of the Queen than has yet appeared in the "private" scenes. And the character which is shown is a further surprise.

The Queen's attitude to the women about her was so arbitrary and fierce that not to have included it would have been a distortion. Plomer transfers the episode of the dress from Lady Mary Howard, with whom Essex had a liaison at this time, to Lady Essex. (An account of Essex's minor promiscuities would have detracted from the dramatic enacting of his pretended love for Elizabeth.)

The court dances are revenants from the sixteenth century to a greater extent than the madrigals—less of a rethinking, closer to pastiche. Nevertheless the La Volta is an appropriate tune for the burlesque treatment of it when the Queen appears, grotesquely, in Lady Essex's dress

EX. 46

with added trombone miaows! There is a moving ensemble for the four conspirators, of Scene 2, when the Queen has gone: "Good Frances, do not weep". All the music sung by and about Lady Essex displays this tender, womanly style, in revealing contrast with the Queen's style. Where Essex's true affections lie is made plain both by this ensemble and by his outburst at the end of it—"[The Queen's] conditions are as crooked as her carcass!" But he is soon to be disarmed. The Queen returns with her Council in full dignity. The notes to which he sang "her conditions . . ." persist, suspiciously, throughout the Queen's preamble until she announces that she has made him "Lord Deputy in Ireland"—the "favour now for every fool" phrase.

The apposition of these two incidents is a strong dramatic stroke. We are, as I have said, surprised to find such an intimate exposure of Elizabeth's weaknesses in such a public

scene. They by no means cancel each other out. The first
incident is very understandable, although repulsive. The
second—the appointment of Essex to Ireland—is puzzling.
On the surface it is a gesture of generosity, to make amends
for the dress incident. It is also an admission of weakness—
"your plainings I can ne'er refuse"—Elizabeth certainly
made the appointment against her better judgement. It
might subconciously have been a trap: "Exalted high among
his peers, he may at last more steeply fall." Contrary to the
apparent implication of the disposition of the Elizabeth and
Essex conversations in the opera—there are none in this act—
the first act is now seen to be an exposition of the typical, the
second a development of the personal manner of the Queen.

The spectacle of dancing was a minor theme unifying the
second act. Two of the third-act scenes are linked by the
portrayal of gossip—the function of this is to spread the effect
and implications of Essex's behaviour so that the Queen (like
Vere in *Billy Budd*) cannot make a private decision about it.
Act III, Scene 1, opens with the Maids of Honour in fluttering
chatter:

What news from Ireland? What news from Ireland?
Delay, delay: a sorry farce!
The summer wasted then a truce!

It is a delicate but worldly picture of the women's environment, showing them living at second hand because of their
closely guarded position, identifying themselves, but not
uncritically, with the Queen.

Essex bursts in upon this harem, a larger-than-life figure,
"wildlooking and travelstained, his hand on his sword". It is
a breath of reality in their second-hand world. But when
Essex forces his way in upon the Queen, she, "wearing an old,
plain dressing-gown . . . as yet without her wig", is the
reality and Essex shrinks to the stature of a romantic gesture.
His subdued greeting:

EX. 47

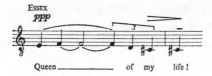

is an echo, lower by a major ninth, of his exuberant cry in the
lute song scene, but he soon rekindles his "flashing gallantries
of the past" in expanding phrases. In contrast to this the
Queen's music is dignified and direct:

EX. 48

After a brief quarrel Essex tries to invoke the lute song (pre-
faced by another appeal "Queen of my life", this time at the
original pitch and screwed up with the original tense har-
monies beneath it). The repeated heavy C minor chords
cannot reawaken the Queen's love—or weakness—and they
sing "Happy were we" in an intensity of regret. It is the last

thing we hear Essex sing. Aptly, the extended cadence is interrupted by the "cares of state" theme. To its notes, the Queen
dismisses Essex to "eat, drink and refresh you . . ." We
cannot know that this very temporary dismissal is the occasion
of our seeing Essex for the last time. It is full of hope. The
condemned Essex is deliberately excluded from the stage in
case his tragedy either alienates our sympathy for or distracts
our attention from Gloriana herself.

A minor version of the homage theme (muted trombone)
perhaps indicates the Queen's acceptance of the "cares of
state"; it is with the same (transposed) notes that she rejected
Essex's love in her soliloquy in the first act, in favour of the
burden and glory of sovereignty, and, in this same version, in
the last scene of the opera she defends her right to execute
Essex to Essex's wife: "A Prince is set upon a stage Alone in
sight of all the world, Alone and must not fail."

This weighty and highly significant music is soothed away
in "The Dressing Table Song": superb lyrical relief, and
restoration of the harem environment, so that Cecil's subsequent entrance contrasts in its propriety with Essex's
intrusion. The major opening of the homage theme makes its
own contrast with the minor one discussed above. There is a
nice historical touch when Elizabeth sings, "What fear is, I
never knew", which we are probably intended to set against
Essex on the scaffold, who confessed that "more than once, in
battle, he had 'felt the weakness of the flesh, and therefore in
this great conflict desired God to assist and strengthen him' ".
The music returns to the "cares" motif at the Queen's "What
say our faithful eyes and ears?" as it did in Act I. This phrase
is incorporated in "Cecil's Report", a typically busy and
unsensational number.

There is a new reminiscence in the "Discussion" that
follows: the interlocked fifths to which the Queen sang
"Victory and Peace" when she appointed Essex lord Deputy,
are reversed in her phrase "think of the waste, count up the

E

cost". The original falling shape of the fifths is roughly delineated in the brass accompaniment to this passage, and permeates the recitative of "The Queen's Decision". Predictably the "cares of state" accompany the breaking of Essex, at the close of the scene. It is a balanced construction: the informal feminine chatter preceding Essex's informal interview with the Queen; the formal "Dressing Table Song" preparing for Cecil's official conversation. Now, in the third act, every time we see the Queen it is in unique and specific situations, which are conducted in the "private" language of the opera. The dramatic shape of the work is beginning to emerge: the Queen's character was displayed in the first act and developed in the second—the portrait is now becoming detailed and focused.

However, the next scene is probably the most difficult to absorb, musically and dramatically, in the opera. Its chief importance is historical: Essex's last half-hearted attempt at treachery, in which the action follows Strachey very closely, even to the extent of making the would-be revolutionaries shout the syllables "Saw! Tray!" as Strachey describes. We do not see Essex leading his ragged band; because of this the scene falls into place as being background, rather than incident; and we may well feel that this is too late in the drama for another look around at the general scene. On the other hand, it is part of the intentional moving away from Essex as a person, and restores Elizabeth's subjects to the foreground.

The scene is a street in the City of London. A blind Ballad Singer disseminates the news of Essex's rebellion, with current developments fed him by his boy, to the Old Men—the male counterpart of the Maids of Honour. The whole scene is a Rondo, the verses of the ballad dominating and enclosing the score. The musical style is a little confusing here: if the lute song was closer to Purcell than Dowland, this ballad is out of Elizabeth's generation by a wider margin. It is an eighteenth-

century-shaped tune, which might almost have come from
The Beggar's Opera:

EX. 49

The only other substantial material in the scene is the chorus
for the rabble of boys, "Now rouse up all the city"—another
clear, square, definite tune reminiscent this time of the
snappy, memorable children's music in *Noye*. For this scene
Britten has suspended the heroic style of the main drama for a
very specialised and isolated (the colourless Cuffe is the only
character in it we have seen before) glance at another face of
this varied age.

There are, however, two devices which help to incorporate
it in the dramatic progress—the parallel portrayals of gossip
have been mentioned, and, perhaps more immediately perceptible, the continuity of tone colour between the predominantly low male voices of the street scene and those of the
Council at Whitehall which open the next scene. The trombones announce the infinitely sad phrase "Essex is guilty and
condemned to die!" Back among his peers we feel this to be a
tragedy: in the street scene it was merely "news". Strachey
graphically depicts the reasons for the Queen's horror at her
words "To die a traitor. Ah!"—even though this revolting
sentence could not apply to one of Essex's rank. "Cecil's
Warning" ("Do not defer this dreadful duty") has a double

echo from Act I, Scene 2—there his counsel was "procrastina-
tion . . . silence and delay"; here his only fear is of delay in
signing Essex's death-warrant. He sings his Warning to the
notes of the Queen's prayer in that earlier scene, but what
sounded ecstatic in Elizabeth's self-dedication to duty sounds
petty and nagging in Cecil's song.

The Council are dismissed to a last canonic trombone
statement of "Essex is guilty". The Queen's aria which
follows reveals the passion she really has for Essex and the
regretful caution which tempers it. It is vivid, noble music,
an aria which could not have occurred any earlier in the
opera, so gradually and progressively has her character been
developed. Penelope, Lady Essex, and Mountjoy now come to
plead for Essex. The smooth arpeggio movement of the melodic lines recalls the conspiracy scene and "Good Frances, do
not weep", and their unanimity of emotion contrasts with the
Queen's dilemma. "Lady Essex's Pleading" is urgent and
informal—over a persistent two-note phrase on Essex's
characteristic clarinets. The Queen makes two replies—as a
Prince, in the minor-key version of the homage theme she
defends her right to condemn Essex; as a woman, in a simple
scale-wise passage she promises to protect his children. The
passage is so short that we can easily miss the fact that the
opera has been developing towards the point where these
contrasted answers both seem equally and utterly characteristic of Elizabeth.

Penelope's pleading is so thoroughly miscalculated that we
realise with a sense of shock that we, by now, know the Queen
better than she—a contemporary—does. It begins as if it is to
be a large-scale (for the proportions of this work) aria, with
brilliant brass and the sweeping "favour" theme in the "out
of favour" version we last heard in "Good Frances": "The
noble Earl of Essex Was born to fame and fortune . . ."
The dotted movement is interrupted when the Queen replies,
"He touched my sceptre, Then he was too great To be en-

dured." Essex's influence, which still distorts her judgement, must be responsible for making the Queen descend to making explanations to Penelope in this manner. But when Lady Rich implies the Earl's independence of the throne—"Still great he would have been, Without the grace and favour of a Queen!"—Elizabeth dismisses her pleading in the music of the dilemma aria into which the episode now flows. Penelope throws out insensitive attempts to arrest the Queen's anger: "He most deserves your pardon Deserves your love", but before the movement ends the Queen signs the warrant.

The frenzied scalic movement of the dilemma aria explodes in a *fortissimo* statement of the second lute song which becomes the musical unit of the Epilogue. This implies a lot. Strachey hints at dating the Queen's decay from the time of Essex's death: "The great reign continued for two years longer, but the pulses of action had grown feeble; and over public affairs there hovered a cloud of weariness and suspense . . . Elizabeth had resisted the first onslaughts of rage and grief with the utmost bravery, but an inevitable reaction followed, and, as the full consciousness of what had happened pressed in upon her, her nervous system began to give way . . . she still worked on at the daily business of government, though at times there were indications that the habits of a lifetime were disintegrating, and she was careless, or forgetful, as she had never been before. To those who watched her it almost seemed as if the inner spring were broken, and that the mechanism continued to act by the mere force of momentum . . . she sat alone, amid emptiness and ashes, bereft of the one thing in the whole world that was worth having. And she herself, with her own hand, had cast it from her, had destroyed it . . ."

It is this sitting alone amid emptiness and ashes, this decline into regret and waking dreams, that Britten and Plomer depict so movingly in the melodrama of the Epilogue. Between the phrases of the lute song, scenes from the last days of Elizabeth's life are spoken, spoken for the most part in actual recorded words which gives an extra layer of intensity to this already tense ending. As her death approaches, the music reaches the bars quoted in Ex. 45—the image of copulation becomes the bodily death of the Queen. The music fades into the last, off-stage, statement of the Homage chorus. The style of the Epilogue is one more part of the immense diversity of language in this diffuse and wide-ranging opera. Like many aspects of the opera, it is a risk—and it succeeds splendidly. One result is an immense tribute to the opera—we find the words of the historical Queen completely consistent with the character of the operatic portrait.

Chapter seven

The Turn of the Screw

Libretto by Myfanwy Piper from the story by Henry James.
First performed September 1954, Teatro La Fenice, Venice.

CHARACTERS

THE GOVERNESS — Jennifer Vyvyan, *soprano*

MRS GROSE, the housekeeper — Joan Cross, *soprano*

PROLOGUE AND QUINT, former man-servant, a ghost — Peter Pears, *tenor*

MISS JESSEL, former governess, a ghost — Arda Mandikian, *soprano*

FLORA ⎫
MILES ⎭ the children — Olive Dyer, *soprano*
David Hemmings, *treble*

Scenery: John Piper
Producer: Basil Coleman
Technical Adviser: Michael Northen
Director of Musical Studies: Hans Oppenheim
General Manager: Basil Douglas

ACT I, PROLOGUE: The Prologue reveals the source of the story, "written in faded ink—a woman's hand", and explains how, at about the middle of the last century, the Governess came to take complete responsibility for the two children at Bly, a country house.

SCENE 1: The Journey. The Governess has misgivings about her lonely position, which she has taken only because she is in love with the children's guardian.

SCENE 2: The Welcome. She arrives and meets Mrs Grose, the housekeeper, and the two children, Miles and Flora.

SCENE 3: The Letter. A letter arrives to inform the Governess that Miles has been expelled from his school.

SCENE 4: The Tower. A summer evening; the Governess sees a figure on the Tower. She immediately thinks it is the guardian, but as she sees him fully she realises that it is a stranger.

SCENE 5: The Window. The Governess sees the stranger again, at the window. She describes him to Mrs Grose, who decides from the description that it is Peter Quint, a former valet who had exerted an evil influence over the household, particularly over the previous governess, Miss Jessel, and Miles—until his death: the Governess only now realises that she has seen a ghost.

SCENE 6: The Lesson. The Governess watches Miles closely to discover signs of Quint's influence, and is disconcerted by what appears to be an uncharacteristic mood, revealed in the Malo song.

SCENE 7: The Lake. The Governess and Flora are by the lake, in the park. The Governess is again alert to suspect Flora of awareness of the ghosts. She sees an apparition of Miss Jessel on the other side of the lake, and believes Flora has seen it, too.

SCENE 8: At Night. The children are discovered in communion with the ghosts.

ACT II, SCENE 1: Colloquy and Soliloquy. Quint and Miss Jessel, "nowhere", plot the moral destruction of the children. The Governess faces her dilemma—uncertain of what is true and what is imagined, and isolated by her friendless position and the guardian's condition forbidding correspondence between them.

SCENE 2: The Bells. It is a Sunday and before morning service. Outside the church Miles challenges the Governess— "Does my uncle think what you think?" She decides to abrogate her responsibilities and leave Bly.

SCENE 3: Miss Jessel. The Governess returns to the schoolroom; she finds Miss Jessel sitting at her desk. Filled now with indignation against the ghosts, rather than frustration with the children, she writes to their guardian: "I have not forgotten your charge of silence, but there are things that you must know."

SCENE 4: The Bedroom. The Governess tells Miles that she has written to his guardian. Just when she is leading Miles towards a confession, Quint's voice is heard, dominating and threatening Miles. The candle goes out (Quint, Miles, or an accident?) and the interview is at an end.

SCENE 5: Quint. Urged by Quint, Miles takes the letter.

SCENE 6: The Piano. Miles entertains the Governess and Mrs Grose at the piano while Flora disappears.

SCENE 7: Flora. The Governess and Mrs Grose find Flora by the lake. The Governess accuses her of having been with Miss Jessel. Flora denies this and Mrs Grose cannot see the apparition.

SCENE 8: Miles. After a night of Flora's dreams, Mrs Grose, now convinced of some precocious evil in the girl, takes her away to her guardian. The Governess and Miles remain at Bly, and in spite of Quint's materialisation, Miles comes near to confessing all. Quint and the Governess do battle over him, and as the boy names Quint he (Miles) collapses in the Governess's arms, dead.

The Turn of the Screw was first performed in Venice in September 1954, the fifth of Britten's chamber operas, to a libretto by Myfanwy Piper from Henry James's story. Like many of Britten's operas, it opens with a Prologue; but the frame is not completed. With an asymmetry rare in any of his works, Britten deliberately leaves the end unspoken as it is in the story—a dramatic device the effect of which we can only assess when we have lived through the suspense of this incredibly gripping work.

It opens, then, with a Prologue: a tenor narrator, accompanied only by the piano, sets the scene in the most matter-of-fact style:

EX. 50

(How impossible it is, even with quotations, to convey the effect of music in words: I challenge anyone to explain why the opening arpeggios sound nostalgic and equally I defy anyone to say that they are not!) One moment in the accompaniment draws attention to itself, both by a sudden *pianissimo* and by a change of pattern—at the words "she was to do everything, be responsible for everything, not to worry him at all, no, not to write . . ." the piano plays rising fourths— a vital interval throughout the opera, here, conspicuous because it is different form the rest of the style of the piano writing in the Prologue.

The scene is set: the governess is engaged to take charge of the two children; and she is forbidden to "worry" her employer—with whom she has fallen instantly in love—with any communication. At this point the opera starts: with the actual words of her consent ("At last, 'I will,' she said"), the orchestra unfolds the Theme which with its fifteen formal variations and sixteen informal ones provides the musical material of the opera. The scheme of the opera is unconventional and can be seen from this plan:

PROLOGUE	ACT II
⎰ Theme ⎱ Scene 1	⎰ Variation VIII ⎱ Scene 1
⎰ Variation I ⎱ Scene 2	⎰ Variation IX ⎱ Scene 2
⎰ Variation II ⎱ Scene 3	⎰ Variation X ⎱ Scene 3
⎰ Variation III ⎱ Scene 4	⎰ Variation XI ⎱ Scene 4
⎰ Variation IV ⎱ Scene 5	⎰ Variation XII ⎱ Scene 5
⎰ Variation V ⎱ Scene 6	⎰ Variation XIII ⎱ Scene 6

$\left\{\begin{array}{l}\text{Variation VI} \\ \text{Scene 7}\end{array}\right.$ $\left\{\begin{array}{l}\text{Variation XIV} \\ \text{Scene 7}\end{array}\right.$

$\left\{\begin{array}{l}\text{Variation VII} \\ \text{Scene 8}\end{array}\right.$ $\left\{\begin{array}{l}\text{Variation XV} \\ \text{Scene 8}\end{array}\right.$

I have bracketed the orchestral variations with the scenes with which they are continuous—many are also continuous with the preceding scenes, but they are invariably connected in mood and usually in matter with the scenes that follow them.

The Theme

EX. 51

Very slow

is a "twelve-note" theme—which is the least important aspect of it in the way it is used in the opera. It consists of a two-bar phrase, its inversion on another set of notes, and a sequence of the inversion. The prominent intervals are rising fourths and dropping fifths. In a way it serves as the orchestral overture (the Prologue being the verbal introduction) with its "French Overture" double dots and ensuing quick movement which uses the rising fourths to dominate the bass line over which a theme is tentatively stated (*fortissimo*, but hidden by the effect of the perpetual motion and hammering rhythm)—a theme which is to become as important to the vocal scenes as Ex. 51 is to the orchestral variations. The bass line (timpani) continues into Scene 1: "The Journey".

The Governess is travelling in a coach towards Bly, expressing her fears and doubts about the situation she has accepted, in short phrases above the continuous pattern of horses' hoofs in the bass. Her fears and the music intensify

when she comes to the verbal point which was made significant in the Prologue: "Whatever happens it is I, I must
decide. A strange world for a stranger's sake"—then at a
sudden *pianissimo* the perpetual motion stops and the Governess sings the important theme that barely emerged from the
rhythmic hammering that introduced the scene:

EX. 52

It appears in various guises throughout the opera, linked
structurally with the Ex. 51 Theme by its filled-in descending
and rising fourths, but it belongs essentially to the scenes, not
the variation-interludes. When it appears in the orchestra it
has the effect of being in quotation marks. It undergoes
numerous changes of rhythm, but usually has a feeling of
impassioned spontaneity which characterises it on this appearance. It cannot be called a motif in that it is not associated
with any single "meaning", although different versions of it
become the personal fingerprints of Quint, Mrs Grose, and
the Governess. It is the very essence of the drama: the situation at Bly brought about by the arrival of the Governess.
To it she sings, "Oh, why, why did I come?" This theme,
which I shall call the Dramatic Theme, reveals gradually
throughout the opera that the drama only comes into being
because the Governess comes to Bly. We have already seen
that the opera starts significantly not with the situation at
Bly but with the Governess's consenting to go there.

The first variation is an uncomplicated movement gradually gathering speed as the children become more impatient
to see their Governess. Superimposed fourths are gradually
built up and become the prevalent chords in Scene 2: "The

Welcome". The children are instantly characterised—as much by what Mrs Grose sings as by their own music. They are surely Britten's most successful operatic children; "period", like the other characters, but incredibly natural in spite of their "possession". Britten and Myfanwy Piper bustle through this scene with a bright daylight, straightforward atmosphere which changes conspicuously when the Governess enters and the strings play the Dramatic Theme to underline the fact that it is her arrival that is to be the catalyst. The scene ends with an ensemble in which Mrs Grose and the children continue to bustle and the Governess sings a lovely expansive melody of interlocking thirds and fourths. She is already transferring her love for the children's guardian to the house and park, as she later transfers it to Miles. Earlier, "A strange world for a stranger's sake"—and already "Bly is now my home!"

The second variation is, like the first, concerned with the children and takes up the rhythm of their exuberant welcome over an extension of the Governess's melody in the last ensemble, emphasising the connection between its intervals and the Theme. The third scene opens calmly, but soon the first news to shatter the Governess's idyll arrives. It is a complicated moment in the drama: to a first-time audience the fact available is that when the Governess reveals that Miles has been expelled from his school the high viola plays the Dramatic Theme, underlining the general uneasiness of the situation; to those who have already heard further on in the opera the celesta motif that colours the first note of this theme is an ironic comment on Mrs Grose's "We were far too long alone"—for the celesta represents the presence of Quint. While Mrs Grose and the Governess are trying to disbelieve the unwelcome letter we see the children singing "Lavenders Blue"—a piece of exaggerated innocence that reassures the grown-ups—and the Governess resolves (to rising fourths) not to write to the guardian to report the dismissal.

Variation III is "sweet summer"—an enchanting tone picture which lulls the audience's apprehensions as the nursery rhyme lulled the Governess's. It is musically continuous with Scene 4, "The Tower". The three phrases of the Theme are transformed into bird-call cadenzas and they are never again in the opera to be heard in so innocent a setting. Again the librettist picks up the word "alone" to use ironically when the character is, in fact, anything but alone. This time it is once more followed by the celesta and now by the apparition of Quint on the Tower. The Governess at first thinks she has seen the children's guardian of whom she has been thinking: not until she has looked fully at him does she realise that it isn't he. She sings:

EX. 53

to an important phrase which tends to recur when she sees the ghosts. The rising fourth is compressed into a shudder and at the same time asks a question which is answered for her not by Quint but by Miles—but this is later.

The grotesque march that is Variation IV seems at first to be imbued with the "Who is it?" shudder, but it is transformed in Scene 5 ("The Window") into an unlikely accompaniment to "Tom, Tom, the Piper's son". This nursery rhyme is sandwiched between two appearances of Quint (as it fades away, he appears at the window, again accompanied by the celesta sound), so that we feel it is at least likely that the children have seen him. When the Governess sees him this time it is the orchestra which asks her question "who is it?" while Mrs Grose elicits a description of Quint from her. Their conversation is punctuated by the orchestral question which fills the Governess's mind.

The next part of the scene—Mrs Grose's narration—is dominated by the phrase:

EX. 54

which is her personal version of the Dramatic Theme and conveys the enacting of the tragedy as it is understood—in a limited way—by her. It is a revelation to the Governess that Quint is dead. She replies, over an agonised version of the Dramatic Theme in major sevenths, "I know nothing of these things, Is this sheltered place the wicked world Where things unspoken of can be?" Later she resolves to protect the children—in an important rhythmic variation of the Dramatic Theme:

EX. 55

which is later associated with her intention and its failure.

Variation V (like I, II and IV) contrasts the apparently uncomplicated world of the children with the problems and doubts of the adults. It is a brisk $\frac{5}{4}$ march from which the tune of Miles's mnemonic song gradually emerges to be sung vigorously in Scene 6, "The Lesson". It seems that this song represents the normal world in which the Governess believes Miles to be living; his second mnemonic song is unexpected stylistically—we have only heard him in this "normal" environment of the Welcome, the nursery rhymes, and the first mnemonic. Now he sings:

EX. 56

Its impact is disturbing, but difficult to define. Certainly it
shows hidden depths in Miles—the style of the music, not the
words. Certainly the defiance of his "I found it, I like it, do
you?" is sung to the music in which he later challenges the
Governess with his "badness" ("you see, I am bad", Scene 8
of the first act; and "Twas I who blew it, dear" in Act II,
Scene 4). Possibly, however, the song represents the ambivalence of his character, not his "possession" by Quint: "I
would rather be . . . in an apple tree . . . than a naughty
boy . . ."—does this song reveal Miles as an *unwilling* victim?

Variation VI effects a link between phrases of the "Malo"
song and Flora's complementary scene, "The Lake". This
shows unsuspected depths in Flora. After a fragment of a
reciting song, paralleling Miles's, she startles the Governess
by naming the lake in the park "The Dead Sea", though
half-reassuring her by declaring "I wouldn't go in it and
neither would Miles"—at this point the oboe refers to "Malo"
emphasising the close symapthy between the children. Flora
then sings a lullaby for her doll which is capable of several
interpretations: there is an element of spell-casting about the
phrase "Dolly must sleep wherever I choose", which we
remember when later to the same music Flora lulls Mrs Grose
to sleep in order to slip out to be with Miss Jessel. Flora's doll,

in this light, takes on the aspect of a "familiar" and it is
ominous that we see her clutching the doll when she goes
away at the end of the opera. She sings a fantastic lullaby
that does nothing to destroy the impression of magic. The
stage directions are important here—Flora "turns round
deliberately to face the audience as Miss Jessel appears at the
other side of the lake"—until the next scene we have no proof
that the children are communicating with the ghosts, although
we do see the ghosts patently pursuing the children. The
Governess, however, thinks Flora has seen the ghost. The
timpani shout her question "Who is it?" (Ex. 53) as she
hurries Flora away, and she sings the version of the Dramatic
Theme in which she expressed her resolve to protect the
children (Ex. 55) to the words "I neither save nor shield
them, I keep nothing from them, O, I am useless". From
this point in the opera this rhythmic version of the theme is
associated with her failure rather than her intention to succeed in protecting the children. At the end of the scene she
sings,

EX. 57

They are   lost!__   lost!__.

the dropping fourth filled in with a portamento, anticipating
with a deep verbal and musical significance the new variant
of the Dramatic Theme which appears in the next variation
and scene.

The celesta ushers in Variation VII before the Governess
has finished singing. In a dialogue between the celesta and
the gong (which characterises the appearances of Miss Jessel)
across a horn statement of the Theme of the variations we
feel the forces gathering for the act finale. The result is very
beautiful music for a conversation between "horrors". In the

following scene, which opens with Quint's cadenza-like variation of the Dramatic Theme, we hear him seduce Miles with
music of sensuous enchantment:

EX. 58

Throughout the opera we hear Quint only through Miles's
ears. If Quint were intended to be a figment of the Governess's imagination—which is a possible interpretation of the
Henry James story and has been used in a production of
this opera which I have not seen—then surely we would
hear him through the Governess's ears, as a menace, not a
hero. Miles responds to Quint with phrases characterised by
the falling portamento; he seizes upon the easily attractive
words "gold", "secrets"—obviously not fully understanding
the compact that is offered him.

Miss Jessel appears, too, her music sharply differing from
Quint's in its deeply tragic line. She is the concrete evidence
of the threat of Quint: his earlier, discarded victim. There is
a continuity in the actions of Quint the man and Quint the
ghost that contradicts the idea that it is the supernatural in
the drama that is frightening. The ghost of Quint is a "devil"
because Quint was one when he was alive. Miss Jessel isn't:
she is a tragedy, though we must believe, if we are aware of
Flora's fate as presenting the "extra turn of the screw", that
she is as menacing to Flora as Quint is to Miles. Her melodic
line is full of heavy minor sevenths, graceless beside Quint's.
Flora responds in the same way that Miles does. This scene is
indeed the climax of the Act—for the first time in the opera
we are sure of the situation: we see the children and the

ghosts together, we also see the real conflict begin with the intervention of Mrs Grose and the Governess, swelling the ensemble momentarily to an unusually thick block of sound. The Theme of the interludes is heard in the bass. The ghosts disappear to the "who is it?" phrase which Miles answers, musically and dramatically—

EX. 59

The second act begins with a substantial introduction, Variation VIII. Between swelling, sustained chords, individual instruments and pairs of instruments have free cadenzas, mostly based on phrases we have heard in Act I—for example, the (literally) haunting canon based on the phrase "The long sighing flight of the night wing'd bird" from the last scene of Act I. The variation ends with a timpani statement of the Theme. Scene 1 takes place "nowhere" and is a colloquy between Quint and Miss Jessel, followed by a soliloquy for the Governess. Quint spurns Miss Jessel and claims a new friend:

> Obedient to follow where I lead,
> Slick as a juggler's mate to catch my thought,
> Proud, curious, agile, he shall feed
> My mounting power
> Then to his bright subservience I'll expound
> The desp'rate passions of a haunted heart,
> And in that hour "The Ceremony of Innocence is
>   Drowned".

Yeats's pregnant phrase is an apt culmination to Quint's macabre plotting. It is taken up by Miss Jessel—who also requires "a soul to share [her] woe"—and is set to a jagged, determined transformation of the Dramatic Theme. The important variations of this theme are rhythmic ones: the Governess's initial "O why did I come?" uses a fluid, meditative shape, loosely but recognisably copied by the orchestra in the letter scene (Scene 3). It is tentative because the shape of the drama, the nature of the conflict, is at this stage only vaguely defined. When the Governess later uses the same notes to express her resolve to "see what I see, know what I know, that they may see and know nothing", the phrase is impelled by an impetuous passion which turns to despair when she sings, to the same notes, "O, I am useless!" Mrs Grose's variant, "Dear God! is there no end to his dreadful ways", is remarkable for mirroring exactly the intonation of the spoken words. It also turns "Dear God" into a deeply felt expostulation that can be detached from the rest of the phrase, and by inverting and evening out the last notes the theme is made to convey the surfeit of horror which has at that point in the story been hers alone. Quint's melismatic summons on the same notes evokes the irresponsibility of all evil, as well as the enchanting arts of the seducer. Here, at "The Ceremony of Innocence is Drowned", the most recent variation of the Dramatic Theme, we see another dimension of Quint—his firm purpose of destruction. The music is tremendously compelling; it compells Miss Jessel, and they sing together, to the Theme of the variations, their joint intention to destroy and possess the children.

The second part of the scene shows the Governess "lost in her labyrinth", reminiscent of Vere in his "cursed mist". She sings "innocence you have corrupted me" and we are reminded that by this stage it is her innocence that is at stake rather than the children's. Her aria ends, "lost in my labyrinth which way shall I turn?" and as if in answer, Variation IX immediately opens with church bells—though they, of course, only sound to a variation of the Theme.

Scene 2, "The Bells", continues with the bells and against

them Flora and Miles, walking to church, sing a most unholy Benedicite with ominous references to phrases from the ghosts' songs ("o ye paths and woods, praise him"), and haunts ("O ye moon and stars, windows and lakes . . ."). Most people's knowledge of this very comprehensive canticle is hazy enough for the "wrong words" to dawn only slowly upon them. The Governess, in this scene, is still in her labyrinth of confusion, dazed with the horror which she refuses to communicate to the children's guardian: "that his house is poisoned, the children mad" (to a phrase from the Dramatic Theme). Miles stays behind with the Governess when Flora and Mrs Grose go in to church. After the closing scene of Act I everything is acknowledged between them, and Miles challenges the Governess with their shared knowledge and the fact that she has not yet written to his guardian, which makes her almost an accomplice. She resolves to leave Bly to a "flight" phrase of a rising fourth which becomes continuous semiquaver movement in Variation X—depicting the flight she does not make. The semiquaver movement in this variation is under-laid by a strongly rhythmic presentation of the Theme which prepares us for the fact that the Governess cannot bring her-self to leave Bly and, in fact, Scene 3 ("Miss Jessel") finds her back in the schoolroom, with Miss Jessel sitting at her desk.

Up to this point I feel that Britten has failed to establish as clear and memorable a musical character for Miss Jessel as for Quint. This perhaps has a dramatic purpose: the opera is concerned with working out the Quint/Miles alliance, and the Miss Jessel/Flora relationship is deliberately left un-finished, just as so many essential facts in the story are left unspoken. However, Miss Jessel's music in Act I, Scene 8, and even in the colloquy (Act II, Scene 1) is indefinite from a characterisation point of view—and possibly this again is a deliberate dramatic device—it is not until this scene in the schoolroom, a milieu which obviously means much to Miss Jessel and to the Governess, that her personality fully unfolds.

It is Miss Jessel's challenge ("I shall come closer and more often, So I shall be waiting, hov'ring, ready for the child") which makes the Governess stay; it was Miles's challenge, in the churchyard, that almost drove her to go. After Miss Jessel disappears (to a most heart-breaking cry: we have mixed reactions to her, hating the unholy power she shares with Quint, yet we cannot withhold sympathy from one of the most tragic ghosts in all opera), the Governess at last writes to the children's guardian. We feel her relief in doing so. This is one of the loveliest moments in the opera. While the Governess writes her letter the orchestra plays an agitated passage, the hesitant, repeated phrases of which are revealed to be the letter itself which the Governess sings as she rereads it in a calmer version. The music indicates that it is a declaration of love coloured with a pathetic hopelessness; her last communication with her employer carried overtones of marriage ("At last 'I will' she said") which account in some degree for her deep involvement with the situation at Bly.

Variation XI is a dialogue between a meditative theme based on interlocking rising fourths and a flurrying arpeggio figure; the whole movement is carried out loosely in canon between bass clarinet and bass flute. That the striking tone colour of these instruments continues through the alternating tempi indicates that the strife is, so to say, a civil one: the altercation is going in on one mind, and the following scene "The Bedroom", reveals this mind to be Miles's. One dramatic point which we can perhaps read into the score is that the flurrying bars are set in motion by a glockenspiel note. Now the celesta represents very much the actual presence of Quint (even when it is used ironically in the letter scene)—and he is not now present. The glockenspiel sounds somewhat akin to the celesta—recollected in agitation. Since Quint is obviously the cause of Miles's mental turmoil, this variation can be shown to display quite audibly the motivation of his thoughts.

Scene 4 continues the flurrying figure, calmed into a gnawing, slow trill through which the Malo song emerges, eventually to be sung by Miles. The scene continues to be a dialogue, but between Miles and the Governess. The Governess is associated with the slow rising fourths which began the variation, and Miles with a new harp figure. The Governess fails to draw any more out of Miles than she has on previous occasions. Just when it seems she might possibly succeed, the music returns to the opening of Variation XI and at the fourth bar, to the glockenspiel plus flurrying phrase is added the voice of Quint, unseen, warning Miles. When the duel—in Miles's mind—between Quint and the Governess threatens to become intolerable, the candle goes out; the Governess sings, "Oh, what is it?" to her earlier "who is it?" phrase, and Miles replies as assertively as he does at the end of Act I, Scene 6, and Act I, Scene 8, and to the same music (EX. 59): "Twas I who blew it, dear."

Variation XII is the only one to include the voice. Quint projects into Miles's mind questions about the letter the Governess has written. Quint's whispered phrases are accompanied by sustained wind chords and side drum with brush chatterings, and are interwoven with an agitated pizzicato development of the Malo song. In the short scene 5, Miles takes the letter. The cor anglais reference to Malo at the end suggests he may already regret it.

Variation XIII—something of a shock until we have seen the ensuing scene—is mock Mozart. A piano movement full of the perverted grace the Governess now sees in Miles. Scene 6 ("The Piano") reveals this to be Miles indeed playing to the Governess and Mrs Grose. This scene shows Miles as enchanter, imitating Quint. In spite of her knowledge, the Governess is bewitched into inattention. Flora weaves a more potent spell: while playing "cat's cradle" she lulls Mrs Grose asleep with a fragment of the lullaby she sang to her doll in Act I, Scene 7—and slips out to join Miss Jessel. Miles, as the Governess subsequently declares, is "with Quint". Variation XIV is a continuation of his piano solo; his character no longer scaled down to the facet of it he presents to the grownups, Miles plays a triumphant paeon. For the first time in the opera we have devilish music, and it continues ominously into Scene 7.

Flora is found by the lake again. The Governess has no hesitation in pointing out Miss Jessel both to Flora and to Mrs Grose. Mrs Grose cannot see the ghost: Flora will not—and sings a childish yet hysterical rejection of the Governess in the middle of which a portamento phrase, "I hate her", recalls the children's style of talking to the ghosts in Act I, Scene 8, and Act II, Scene 2. It is this phrase that the Governess broods over at the end of the scene. She sings the Dramatic Theme to the words, "But I have failed, most miserably failed and there is no more innocence in me".

Variation XV begins with similar big chords to those which swelled and subsided in Variation VIII. These do not subside. They explode first in a falling piccolo phrase, then in a rising timpani phrase (which dies away in a glissando). It has the effect of intolerably intensifying the mood for the climax of the opera. Scene 8 opens with the phrase in which the Governess sang "My friend, you have forsaken me at last" in the previous scene. Mrs Grose and Flora are about to depart—this is the last time we are to see Flora, and it is full of echoes: she is holding her doll, which has by now strong supernatural connotations, and when "the Governess walks towards them, Flora deliberately turns her back"—in the Act I lake scene it was from Miss Jessel that she deliberately turned. Mrs Grose, however, has not forsaken the Governess after all. The orchestra reveals that she is able to see the nightmarish period she has spent with Flora as an extension of Quint's influence: "Dear God, is there no end to his dreadful ways?" This theme (Ex. 54) is played a second time when they discover that Miles has stolen the letter. Mrs Grose and

Flora go away, but it is with no sense of optimism that we see them leave: nothing that we have been shown of the guardian or Mrs Grose during the opera gives the impression that they will be capable of dealing with a situation that has defeated the Governess.

As they go the last movement starts—a passacaglia—with the Theme of the variation interludes as its bass. The Governess again sings the Dramatic Theme, this time confidently: "O Miles, I cannot bear to lose you. You shall be mine and I shall save you". But because this theme has been associated so cumulatively with her failure, we know already that she will not succeed. The passacaglia—almost inevitable for a Britten opera climax—is a very effective way of conveying the fact that things are moving at last. It has been a static opera until this point. The situation is no different from the beginning, except that the Governess knows about it. We have no evidence to suggest that Miles and Flora are more deeply embroiled than when they first welcomed the Governess with unnatural charm.*

The measured walking pace of the repeated bass is purposeful. The Governess's tentative conversation with Miles is full of suspense and verbal fencing:

MILES: So my, dear, we are alone.
GOVERNESS: Are we alone?
MILES: O, I'm afraid so.
GOVERNESS: Do you mind being left alone?
MILES: Do you?
GOVERNESS: Dearest Miles, I love to be with you.
   What else should I stay for?

We have been here before—and got no further—but the rhythm of the music is gradually moving forward. When the

* I have seen a production in which Quint appears in fetters at the beginning of the opera; these fall half off when Miles steals the letter and are gone in the last scene. It is an interesting idea, but unjustified in the text. Miles is dismissed his school before the opera starts.

Governess asks, ". . . tell me, what it is then you have on your mind", Quint joins the ensemble (as he did in the bedroom scene) answering her by his presence when Miles will not. Miles is the central (though by this stage, silent) figure in the struggle between the Governess and Quint, to possess him. At the climax of their duet, perhaps a surprisingly quiet climax, Miles turns on Quint, names him, and dies. To the phrase which has been used for Miles's enigmatic answers and challenges (Ex. 59) Quint bids him farewell; he disappears to the first lovely melisma he sang in Act I, Scene 8. The Governess meanwhile, does not realise that Miles is dead. "Ah, Miles, you are saved," she sings. "Now all will be well", and, ironically, "Together we have destroyed him." When she discovers she is holding the dead child she sings, passionately, the Malo song, which concludes the opera.

The Turn of the Screw is, I think, with *Billy Budd*, Britten's finest opera up to the present. This subject could only be set within the intimacy of chamber opera: the oppressive intimacy of Bly which the guardian had tasted and shunned is made a reason for the close-knit structure of the work. The lack of development in the story—in so great a contrast to *Billy Budd*—is solved by the episodic form. The setting of the very skilful libretto is so clear and sensitive that the characters —not one of whom is in any way ready-made or an operatic type—are consistent in every phrase that they sing: Miles, for example, sings so little, yet by the lesson scene we are already able to recognise the inconsistency of the Malo song —and to speculate on its significance.

Chapter eight

Noye's Fludde

Libretto from the Chester Miracle Plays.
First performed Orford Church, June 1958.

CHARACTERS

THE VOICE OF GOD — Trevor Anthony, *spoken*
NOYE — Owen Brannigan,
    bass-baritone
MRS NOYE — Gladys Parr, *contralto*
SEM — Thomas Bevan, *treble*
HAM — } their sons — { Marcus Norman, *treble*
    { Brian Weller
JAFFETT — Michael Crawford, *tenor*
MRS SEM — Janette Miller }
MRS HAM — Katherine Dyson } *girl sopranos*
MRS JAFFETT — Marilyn Baker, }

CHORUS OF GOSSIPS — Penelope Allen }
    Doreen Metcalfe } *girl sopranos*
    Dawn Mendham }
    Beverley Newman }

THE RAVEN — David Bedwell, *dancer*
THE DOVE — Maria Spall, *dancer*
THE CONGREGATION

The chorus of Animals and the Orchestra were from East Suffolk schools with the English Opera Group Players, leader Emanuel Hurwitz.

Production and setting: Colin Graham
Costumes: Ceri Richards
Conductor: Charles Mackerras
Assistant Conductor: Jan Cervenka

After the congregational hymn, "Lord Jesus, think on me", the voice of God announces to Noye that He intends to punish the wickedness of man by destroying the earth in a flood. Noye, his wife, their three children, and their wives are to be saved. God gives Noye instructions for building the Ark, and work commences—in spite of the mockery of Mrs Noye and her companions. The Ark is finished, but Mrs Noye still refuses to take the threatened flood seriously. The animals are brought into the Ark. Noye's sons go to persuade their mother to enter the Ark and eventually have to carry her into it! They close the Ark and the storm begins. At the height of the storm the congregation sings "Eternal Father, strong to save".

After the storm Noye sends a raven out of the Ark. It does not return—a sign that it has found dry land. Then he sends a dove: the dove returns with an olive branch, a sign of fertile conditions. God commands Noye and his family to leave the Ark and creates the rainbow as a symbol of His future goodwill to mankind. The congregation sings "The spacious firmament on high".

Noye's Fludde is one of a cycle of medieval plays known as the Chester Miracle Plays. These formed an essentially civic and lay celebration of religious festivals. The plays were performed by individual Guilds, acting on floats which processed around the town performing in the market-place and outside the church door—the important thing being that the performances took place outside the churches, unlike the liturgical drama from which they derived. Although they continued as late as the sixteenth century, and it is on a sixteenth-century text that this opera is based, their entire spirit is that of the Middle Ages: the wilful anachronisms and the vitality of the vernacular expression of religious ideas combine to present us with characters as idiosyncratic as Chaucer's, clearly deriving from the people who created the roles in the dramas.

Britten re-creates the sense of communal activity of the Miracle plays. *Noye's Fludde* involves a wide range of singing activity and an even greater instrumental diversity. Among the large range of instruments, some are more equal than others: "the orchestra is of two kinds, professional and children (amateurs) . . . There are three sorts of amateur violins: the *firsts* should be capable players, not however going above the 3rd position, and with the simplest double-stops. The *seconds* do not go out of the 1st position, while the *thirds* are very elementary, and have long stretches of just open strings . . ." (Preface). Even the audience is fully involved, and is, in fact, responsible for the climaxes of the opera. The whole orchestral force is: Professional—solo string quintet, solo treble recorder, piano duet, organ and timpani; Children—string orchestra, recorders, bugles, handbells, bass, tenor and side drums, tambourine, cymbals, triangle, whip, gong, Chinese blocks, wind machine, sandpaper scrapers, and "tuned" suspended mugs.

The work opens with a setting of the hymn "Lord Jesus, think on me", sung by the audience (designated "congregation", for Britten's re-creation, unlike the original, is intended to be performed in church). It is a fierce, penitential opening, the sort of setting which, once we have heard it, makes the "normal" use of this hymn unbearably tame. The melodic and rhythmic shape of the hymn is used in a number of contexts in the opera. The key phrase of the setting, timpani rolls and the bass line of the first two bars, becomes the accompaniment to God's voice, a spoken part. This phrase recurs to underline the 3 + 1 shape of the verse:

I, God, that all this worlde hath wroughte,
Heaven and eairth, and all of naughte,
I see my people in deede and thoughte,
Are sette full fowle in synne.
Man that I made I will destroye,
Beaste, worme and fowle to flye,
For on eairth they me deny,
The folk that are theiron.

When God gives the very practical information of the dimensions of the ark, Noye joins in, as if taking notes, and the rhythm gradually speeds up into the busy music of the "Building of the Ark".

Each section of the opera has a prevailing instrumental colour: this is predominantly piano and string tone. Noye's children (three trebles and three girl sopranos) have memorable material

EX. 60

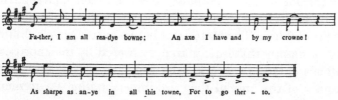

Fa-ther, I am all rea-dye bowne; An axe I have and by my crowne!

As sharpe as an-ye in all this towne, For to go ther - to.

It is enchanting music. The vigour and rhythmic life completely reflect the medieval mood and diction. Probably in no previous century since the original could this play have been set in a musical style so apt for this verbal and conceptual climate of thought.

The entry of Mrs Noye and her "gossips" provides a comic interlude, characteristic of the Miracle plays. She sings the children's building music in mocking augmentation and a spirit of non-cooperation. Her gossips repeat it in chattering double diminution. Noye and the children begin to build the ark, Noye singing a short strophic air:

EX. 61

This is a closely knit movement; the bass moves in rising fifths, a big extension of Noye's first interval, with phrases from "Lord Jesus, think on me" sung at the cadences by the children. The unity is surprising. The style of the music for the adult singers closely conforms with that of the children, but this simplicity is effected without losing any musical opportunities.

God's voice interrupts further squabbling between Noye and Mrs Noye. It is accompanied similarly to its first appearance and again its spacious, non-urgent style is transformed by Noye—an embryo Moses—into purposeful action. This is the episode of the "Animals", bugle fanfares characterising the orchestral sound, and introducing another splendid tune for the children. The material is in two parts: Noye's children have a snappy rhythmic march, answered by the choruses of animals entering the ark, who sing "Kyrie eleison" in the manner of the animal they are impersonating—a tremendously vital act of worship and an exciting dramatic effect.

There is another Mrs Noye episode, in which the first line of the opening hymn is again recalled, again cadentially. Sem goes to persuade Mrs Noye to enter the ark and is rebuffed. The gossips sing a drinking song to drown their fear of the flood. It is another number of very direct expression in which the character of the gossips is unambiguously identifiable:

EX. 62

The verses are interspersed with more pleas from Noye. Eventually his sons carry their mother bodily into the ark.

The episode of the "Storm" begins, involving particularly percussion* and recorders. The whole section is a passacaglia over this rising four-bar phrase:

EX. 63

Noye's children and Mrs Noye sing a rhythmically altered version of the opening hymn; then they shut themselves in the ark and the orchestra takes over for an extended instrumental passage, the longest in the work. A climax slowly develops and out of a long rising chromatic scale (which helps

---

* The slung mugs make a remarkably wet sound. I played this to a four-year-old who had not much idea of what was going on and she instantly identified them as raindrops.

the assimilation of the harmonic style of the hymn) the central hymn, "Eternal Father, strong to save", emerges, and is sung by the congregation, still with the passacaglia bass. The storm then subsides, working loosely backwards through the material with which it was built up.

"After the Storm"—the two birds Noye sends to prospect for dry land are characterised in dances: the raven with a solo cello, a seeking, restless chromatic movement; the dove with a solo recorder cooing caressingly. Noye's recitative is accompanied by recollections of the storm passacaglia tune. God's voice commands Noye to

> Take thy wife anone,
> And thy children everyone,
> Out of the Shippë thou shalt gone,
> And they all with thee.
> Beastes and all that can flie,
> Out anone they shall hye,
> On eairth to grow and multeplye, .
> I will that soe yt be.

There is another spacious, cumulative ensemble as the animals and "The Noye Family Leave the Ark". The build-up is visual as well as aural. Musically it is based on a third memorable children's tune:

EX. 64

Al - le - lu - ia,— Al - le - lu - ia!

The bugles are prominent again.

The final section of the drama is the "Creation of the Rainbow", and the promise it represents. The music is coloured for the first time by the handbells. The vocal material is a magical union of Tallis and Addison, enriching the already freely anachronistic manner that gives such punch to

medieval expression with layer upon layer of experience: a
post-Newtonian poem set to a sixteenth-century hymn sung
by Noye's family and a twentieth-century audience!

EX. 65

The work is a joy, and remarkable from any point of view.
Britten's music for children has been one of his most influential fields of action and much good primary-school music, in
particular, has been written since this opera. But there have
been few other works where the form itself motivates the
inclusion of children and audience. *Noye's Fludde* succeeds
glowingly—whether we regard it as a community act of
worship or do-it-yourself drama—succeeds as music in which
the assorted limitations of the performers result in unlimited
vitality and apt interpretation of the original.

Chapter nine

A Midsummer Night's Dream

Libretto adapted from Shakespeare by Benjamin Britten and Peter Pears.
First performed Jubilee Hall, Aldeburgh, June 1960.

CHARACTERS

OBERON, King of the Fairies	Alfred Deller, *counter-tenor*
TYTANIA, Queen of the Fairies	Jennifer Vyvyan, *soprano*
PUCK	{ Leonide Massine II, Nicholas Chagrin, *spoken role*
COBWEB, a fairy	Kevin Platts, *treble*
PEASEBLOSSOM, a fairy	Michael Bauer, *treble*
MUSTARDSEED, a fairy	Robert McCutcheon, *treble*
MOTH, a fairy	Barry Ferguson, *treble*
FAIRIES	Thomas Bevan, *treble* Thomas Smyth, *treble*
THESEUS, Duke of Athens	{ Forbes Robinson, *bass* Roger Stalman
HIPPOLYTA, betrothed to Theseus	Johanna Peters, *contralto*
LYSANDER	George Maran, *tenor*
DEMETRIUS	Thomas Hemsley, *baritone*
HERMIA ⎫ young people of Athens	Marjorie Thomas, *mezzo-soprano*
HELENA ⎭	{ April Cantelo, *soprano* Joan Carlyle
BOTTOM, a weaver	{ Owen Brannigan, *bass baritone* Forbes Robinson
QUINCE, a carpenter	Norman Lumsden, *bass*
FLUTE, a bellows-mender	Peter Pears, *tenor*
SNUG, a joiner	David Kelly, *bass*
SNOUT, a tinker	Edward Byles, *tenor*
STARVELING, a tailor	Joseph Ward, *baritone*

Conductors: Benjamin Britten and George Malcolm
Producer: John Cranko
Designers: John Piper and Carl Toms
Stage Director: John Copley

ACT I: The Wood. Oberon and Tytania quarrel over the Indian boy. Oberon dispatches Puck to find a magic herb the juice of which will "make man or woman madly dote Upon the next live creature that it sees", in order to plague his Queen and possess the boy. Lysander and Hermia meet and plan their elopement, to avoid Hermia's betrothal to Demetrius. Overlooked by Oberon, Demetrius enters pursued by Helena: Helena is in love with Demetrius, while he loves Hermia.

Puck returns with the magic herb and Oberon now charges him to use it to make Demetrius enamoured of Helena.

The mechanicals set about casting their play, *Pyramus and Thisby*. Puck mistakes Lysander and Hermia, sleeping, for Demetrius and Helena. He anoints Lysander with the magic juice, but it is Helena, abandoned by Demetrius, who wakes him and as a result of the enchantment Lysander is now utterly in love with Helena. Oberon finds the sleeping Tytania and squeezes the juice on her eyes.

ACT II: The Wood. The mechanicals' rehearsal goes forward. Puck puts an ass's head upon Bottom: unaware, Bottom scares away his companions and wakes the enchanted Tytania— who falls in love with him.

Hermia is abandoned by Lysander and pursued by Demetrius. Oberon enchants Demetrius, who wakes to find Helena. Now both Lysander and Demetrius are in love with Helena, who can be forgiven for thinking that both of them and the spurned Hermia are mocking her.

Oberon gives Puck another herb to disenchant Lysander.

ACT III: The Wood, early next morning. Oberon, satisfied that he has the Indian boy, determines to resolve "this hateful imperfection", disenchants Tytania, and promises to see the "pairs of faithful lovers wedded with Theseus all in jollity".

The lovers awake, now tidily paired—Helena with Demetrius and Hermia with Lysander. Bottom, too, wakes up and, rejoining his crew, makes final preparation for their play.

At Theseus's Palace, Theseus and Hippolyta are joined by the four lovers and a triple wedding is planned.

The mechanicals present the "lamentable comedy of *Pyramus and Thisby*" for the court's entertainment. Festivities are concluded at midnight, the couples retire, and the fairies return to bless the palace and the nuptials.

There are problems in turning a well-known original play into an opera which do not exist in ordinary circumstances—which did not exist, for example, in *Peter Grimes*, *Billy Budd*, or *Gloriana*. To convert any familiar story into opera is difficult enough, since the librettist must tamper with the emphasis and the composer with the proportions in order to present the drama in terms of music. But a play looks misleadingly like a libretto, and with a celebrated Shakespearean play the very knowledge on the part of the audience of passages of the text, end-of-scene couplets, and the general structure may set up barriers between their acceptance of "a new version with music" and their reverence for "the real thing". An opera must, then, radically change the original if only for its own survival. *A Midsummer Night's Dream* (Britten) has a number of things in common with *A Midsummer Night's Dream* (Shakespeare), but it presents a single interpretation of the comprehensive material of the play, and in imposing this narrow reading reveals some aspects in compensatingly greater depth.

The *Dream* is not the most potentially operatic play of Shakespeare's: *Othello* and *Macbeth* are the obvious stuff on which nineteenth-century operas, at least, are made. As Comedy, the *Dream* has strong traditional conventions which have grown up quite separately from traditional comic opera —there is not only no correspondence between comic opera and comic drama, but also both have developed highly idiomatic approaches to comedy which have to be reinterpreted during the transformation. (For example, there is nothing in the play to direct what musical change of style should be used for the *Pyramus and Thisby* play, and nothing in the thin annals of English opera to suggest in what way prose should be handled differently from blank verse, and blank verse from rhymed.) In short, the experience of the *Dream*—the most English of the comedies—is the most unlikely experience to find in opera, of our time, in this country.

So there are changes. Opera is a blunt instrument: opera tends to simplify rather than compress. The Theseus/Hippolyta frame of the play has been removed; Theseus appears only at the end, as a rather tin god to overrule Hermia's father and arrange the weddings. That he is not the real *deus ex machina* we have become very aware during the course of the opera. This is the role of faery in the opera. The faeries, the most essentially Oberon, are the controlling force of the drama; they have the most musically extensive style and—in spite of Puck's mishaps—are the most dramatically powerful. They bear little relation to the gossamer creatures of Mendelssohn's incidental music. Britten and Pears set the seal on their interpretation of the play by putting the faeries at the centre of the opera, endowing them with heavy magic and, indeed, implied divinity. They are promoted to the framing role and in consequence "reality" or the norm is shifted from the anachronistic court of Athens to the domestic and cosmic affairs of Tytania and Oberon.

The lovers are patently in their power. And they are diminished by this contact. It is only as lovers that we see them, and yet this intimate core of their natures, the only justification of their appearance in the drama, is so controlled by the use and misuse of Oberon's magic that they appear less than life-size in consequence. Hermia and Helena are drawn on a larger scale than the men: they are, for one thing, constant—they are untouched by the magic, And we do have a fuller picture of them in Helena's aria of their girlhood. But they are as much at the mercy of the men as the men are at the mercy of the magic—and they tend to take their dramatic dimensions from Lysander and Demetrius.

The mechanicals tangle more substantially with the faery world, and through Oberon's careful purpose and the

splendidly arbitrary behaviour of Puck, Bottom is admitted
within it. That he is undiminished by this contact is a special
characteristic of Bottom. His companions are as much at the
mercy of the magic as are the lovers—their play cannot go
forward without Bottom—and a faery whim can shatter their
material world. The opera, then, is concerned specifically
with power: the benign amorality of faery power. By putting
the faeries at the centre of the opera, every other aspect is
seen only as touched by them.

The faery world is more extensive than the Athens of the
mortals and is depicted in more detail. In a sense, all the
scenes which take place in the wood are in "faeryland", but it
is defined in the opera more in terms of sound than space, and
there are a number of special sonorities which admit us into
the presence of the faeries. The first is indicated in the opening
bars of the opera—the mysterious string glissandi—

EX. 66

—which immediately evoke both the other-worldliness and
the power of the faeries. In contrast to this, the harp, invariably, and the harpsichord, sometimes, accompany the scalic
tune of the trebles

EX. 67

—the other-worldliness without the power. Transparent textures, often on a similar scale to the chamber operas, are a feature of the opera (written, after all, for the Jubilee Hall, not Covent Garden: a semi-chamber opera). They are physically necessary to give effective passage to the children's voices and the counter-tenor Oberon; and they exploit the precision of the harpsichord, the intimacy of the solo string writing and the specially magic sound of string and harp harmonics. Puck, a spoken role, has his own sonority in the trumpet and drum accompaniment to his appearances. Oberon's spell—the powerhouse of the whole drama—is evoked in a pattern for the celesta which both condenses and accompanies the melodic line of the spell theme:

EX. 68

The faery characters divide musically into three groups. The first, Cobweb, Mustardseed, Moth, Peaseblossom, and their companions are trebles. Their music is more sophisticated than any earlier children's music in Britten's operas, though it has as always an absolute clarity and directness in the structure of the tunes that is completely apt for the voices. Ex. 67 shows Britten's rhythms working, as they must, quite independently of the verbal rhythms—a fact which it is far easier to appreciate than to achieve for oneself! Ex. 67 recurs and is always associated with contrasting chordal tunes. At the end of the first act it appears, inverted, as a lullaby refrain to "You spotted snakes", which spans the same major sixth range with arpeggio movement instead of step-wise. These faeries are appurtenances to Tytania and range themselves whole-heartedly on her side in the quarrel with Oberon. Their

blind obedience to her, even in her scene with Bottom, is
amply illustrated in the mechanical little phrase with which
they greet Bottom:

EX. 69

Hail,   hail,   mor-tal, hail,   mortal, mortal, hail,   hail.

They possess no power—or if they do it is of a very inferior
order: their elaborate charm ("You spotted snakes") at the
end of the first act, and even their sentinel left on guard,
cannot prevent Oberon's approach. Intervals of thirds and
sixths are prevalent in the faery music. This group explores
parallel thirds, moving chromatically, in the soothing "On
the ground, sleep sound" chorus which closes the second act;
and a pair of these thirds, as it were uncoiled, introduce the
closing section of the whole opera in a more intricate line:

EX. 70

Now, now the hungry li-on roars And the wolf behowls the   Moon, whilst the hea-vy ploughman

snores, All with wear-y task for   done.

These faeries are essentially lyrical beings: to sing—tunes—is
their service to Tytania and they guard her, lull her and
entertain her guest with characteristically melodic response.

In contrast to this lyricism, Puck is a spoken part. He is
Oberon's acolyte and the timbre of the spoken voice balances
and combines with the counter-tenor tone in the same way
that the fluently melodic faery chorus is matched with the
coloratura role of Tytania. He is necessarily an acrobat; the
trumpet arpeggio with which he is musically characterised is
always further ranging than the faery group's melodies, and
the high, tuned drum excites more physical action:

EX. 71

Because he is so intimately associated with Oberon he has a share in wielding the magic—he enchants Lysander to a very Puck-coloured version of the spell. His instrumentally exuberant nature is only suppressed when Oberon is angry with him, after the lovers' central quarrel scene; but he is quite without remorse and the trumpet soon reappears, as he misleads Lysander and Demetrius through the mist. He has the final scene to himself—not an inflated role if we regard him as the executive function of Oberon, who has brought about the entire drama and deserves to wind it up.

There are, in the *play*, always two ways of assessing the part played by Oberon and Tytania: either they are semi-divine spirits whose domestic quarrellings have an effect on the natural order—

TYTANIA: . . . I have forsworn his bed and company.
OBERON: Therefore the winds have sucked up from the sea Contagious fogs,
TYTANIA: Therefore the ox hath stretched his yoke in vain,
OBERON: The fold stands empty in the drowned fields,
TYTANIA: The crows are fatted with the murion flock.
OBERON AND TYTANIA: The seasons alter . . .

who wield a real power over mortals—

When they next wake, all this derision
Shall seem a dream and fruitless vision,

and are worshipped—"his mother was a votress of my Order".

Or, alternatively, we are free to consider them merely a projection of the mortal world; they are invented scapegoats for the "progeny of evils" (the more trivial incidents are attributed to Puck:

Are you not he
That frights the maidens of the villagery,
Skim milk and sometimes labour in the quern,
And bootless make the breathless huswife churn . . .);

they, the faeries, are blamed for the inherent faithlessness of lovers and are dreamed up superstitiously to bless marriages. I think that Britten and Pears, in their adaptation of the play, come down indisputably in favour of the former role. The fact that we have an extended faery scene for the first scene in the opera (they do not appear till the second act in Shakespeare) and, more subtly, that Lysander and Hermia's first scene in the opera takes place in the wood which we have already seen and heard to be an enchanted sphere of action (the lovers and the mechanicals unwittingly seek out contact with the fairies); that, in the opera, Demetrius does not reveal that he was once betrothed to Helena and is in the third act reverting to his "natural taste"—instead in the opera he remains enchanted and in Oberon's power—these facts assert the reality of the faeries and the consequent domination of the music and the drama by their king and queen.

Vocally they are shown to be creatures of a different kind from the mortals; Tytania is a coloratura soprano. It is perhaps a dramatic fault that her voice physically overwhelms Oberon's, since she does not do so dramatically. Possibly, however, she is being punished in the opera as much for her overbearing volume of sound in the first scene as for her refusal to part with the Indian boy: when Oberon passes through the fairy guard to annoint Tytania's eyes with the magic herb, it is her magic he is breaking—magic which is identified with vocal art

EX. 72

and the false security of her guarded sleep is closely linked
with the "roundel and a fairy song" which she commissions.
This point having been established, her devotion to Bottom is
doubly ridiculous, when after his un-lyrical attempt at "The
woosell cock so black of hue", she sings—

> I pray thee, gentle mortal, sing again;
> Mine ear is much enamoured of thy note.

She is vocally subdued when Oberon removes the enchantment, and even when he invites her to summon her music,
she sings a restrained phrase; and in the house-blessing scene
at the close of the opera she is relegated to a line in the
ensemble equivalent to those of her minions:

EX. 73

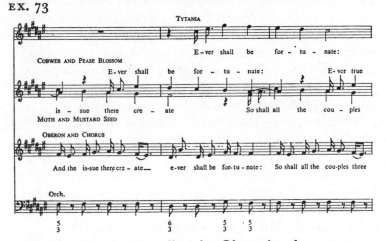

—by this stage they are all under Oberon's rule.

Oberon is the central figure of the opera. He is distinguished vocally from the mortals by being a counter-tenor

which, ideally, ought to bring to the part a cutting clarity of tone to match the harpsichord, celesta, trumpet, and spoken voice associated with his music. Perhaps the existence of this role will generate its own vocally significant exponents; certainly the middle *tessitura* and frequent repeated notes make less sense for the alternative—a contralto voice. Oberon is too vast a character for the limits of motivic characterisation, but an important aspect of his mind is revealed in the spell music (Ex. 68)—a bitonal theme which not only depicts the transforming aspect of the magic but also the devious (and not very responsible) workings of Oberon's mind. This spell absorbs him from the moment of Tytania's refusal to part with the boy. He is brooding on it when he enters to witness Demetrius and Helena's first quarrel. His aria, "I know a bank", is a development and free extension of the spell theme, which is also compressed into a single word, revealingly:

EX. 74

fan – – – ta-'sies

Once he has relieved Tytania of her enchantment these intervals cease to obsess his melodic line and we are shown a more majestic character in the Ex. 73 ensemble—the ritual of magic power rather than the arbitrary and private uses of it.

Oberon's scenes with Tytania are built on a three-note descending figure

EX. 75

Jea-lous O - ber - on
Proud Ty - ta - ni - a

which seems to have the function of focusing the music, after the wide-sweeping glissandi of Ex. 66, on the private and domestic relationship between Oberon and Tytania. It is applied to the following, among a great variety of phrases: "Oberon is passing *fell and wrath*"; "*Jealous Oberon*"; "*Proud Tytania*"; "I have forsworn his bed and *company*". It is used for "*My Oberon!*" (Tytania waking and disenchanted) and inverted for "Now thou and I are *new in amity*" and, as a motif, it seems to belong both to the quarrel and the reconciliation, but not to any exterior concerns of either Oberon or Tytania.

The lovers are limited creatures compared with the faeries. We see them only as lovers—in contact with no one (until the scene at Theseus's court) but their pursued and pursuing interchanging partners. For more than half the time the men are under the spell and the women battling with the irrational treatment they receive. Love is not portrayed as glorious: it is painful, cruel, and, in the end, trivial. There is not much scope for characterisation, since not much character is revealed—or is there to be revealed. All the scenes are based on an aching chromatic phrase

EX. 76

and each of the four lovers derives much of his or her melodic line from this. The only occasions on which the music departs from this material are made significant by its absence. In the first Hermia and Lysander scene the style changes at the vows into a musical as well as verbal hyperbole which indicates the irony of their protestations:

EX. 77

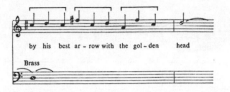

by his best ar - row with the gol - den head

Brass

These vows are doomed because they do not take into account the prevailing state of the four lovers—depicted in Ex. 76: they portray their love as resplendent when, in fact, both Helena and Demetrius are suffering because of it, and they portray it in terms of harmonic solidity when it is sufficiently fickle to be disrupted by a whim—or sufficiently vulnerable to be shattered by faery power.

In Helena and Demetrius's first scene, separated from the vows only by the brief appearance of Oberon, meditating magic, the same pervading theme (Ex. 76) emphasises the interchangeability of the two pairs. While the yearning phrase (a) was strongly associated with the mutual but unfulfilled love of Hermia and Lysander, however, Demetrius expresses his rejection of Helena chiefly in phrase (b), which becomes "I love thee not". Helena expresses her spurned passion in a broken version of phrase (a):

> You draw me . . . you hard hearted . . . adamant . . .
> Leave you your . . . power to draw
> And I shall have no . . . power to follow you.

But she is shown to have some independence of this theme in her two short arias—"I am your spaniel" in this scene and "Injurious Hermia" in the quarrel scene, both of which have a fresh, non-chromatic style which isolates them in their contexts—just as Helena is forced into isolation by Demetrius's treatment of her:

EX. 78

EX. 79

Whenever Lysander breaks free of Ex. 76 we know he is acting uncharacteristically. Under the spell, he wakes to find Helena, and protests his love for her in a quite different style —an impetuous diatonic line with frequent grace notes:

EX. 79

A disturbed string texture is associated with this music—it recurs when Demetrius is, in his turn, enchanted, and his spellbound vocal line augments the tonal alternation in the orchestra:

EX. 80

The men resolve to fight to an inversion of Ex. 76:

> to try whose right
> Of thine or mine is most in Helena.

When in the last act the lovers wake they return, of course, to Ex. 76 material. The pairs are now appropriately differentiated: Lysander and Hermia awake to versions of the (a) phrase which has throughout represented their reciprocated love; Helena to a fragment of (c), which must now represent her new union (since (b) was interpreted as Demetrius's rejection of her). Demetrius's waking phrase is a compromise—the "undiscriminating", enchanted interval of a tone (see Ex. 80) refined into a semitone borrowed from (a)? This does not matter. The lovers are not real enough for it to be a problem that Demetrius remains enchanted—and that Lysander once spurned Hermia so unkindly. The "horns of elfland faintly blowing" mock them throughout this scene. The awakening and the continued enchantment are expressed most aptly in the ensemble

> And I have found Demetrius, like a jewel.
> Mine own, and not mine own.

The glowing harmonic changes refer back to the vows of the first act, but the chastening experiences in the wood result in a less ambitious flaunting of fidelity, and the grace notes recall Ex. 79 and the tenuous control each has over his own or his lover's affections.

If in the play we regard the faery world as a product of the imagination, then the mechanicals are at the very roots of reality. But we cannot, as I have tried to show, view the opera in this way. There is no more potent argument for the objective existence of faery than 'Bottom's Dream"—Bottom's entry into Tytania realm—because this experience could not be the product of his imagination: the scene with Tytania, in the opera, could never have been conceived by Bottom, with the musical character he is given. The function of the mechanicals in the opera is partly to represent in their *Pyramus and Thisby* play another aspect of the confusions of love (and show by implication how much better these things are handled by the faeries: Oberon is the only lover in the drama who extricates himself by his own endeavours from adverse circumstances) and partly to show how all levels of life come into contact with faery magic and are overpowered by it. The range of musical expression in the opera is immense. After all the variety of the faery music, and the intensity of the lovers' scenes, we now have the superb comedy of the mechanicals.

Their first scene depicts the progress of the mood of the rehearsal—from their tentative, diffident entrance to optimistic euphoria. Each of the characters is memorably delineated in this and the subsequent scenes, but two of them, Bottom and Flute, have particularly interesting musical characters. There is this difference between them: Bottom's music interprets his verbal character fully—a considerable feat—but I do not think it adds anything that is not present in the play; Flute, on the other hand, is a shadowy figure in the play, whose main characteristic is to allow himself to be overborne by Bottom and Quince—in the opera he has a detailed musical character which unfolds far more vividly and credibly than it does in the text. Bottom's initial enthusiasm is represented in a phrase to which he sings all the lines he aspires to act:

EX. 81

and   Phi -- bus' car shall shine from far, shall   shine from far   and   make and mar......

—he is still singing this to "This is Ercles' vein, a tyrant's vein" while Flute is being cast as Thisby, and he takes up Thisby's lines to the same tune (falsetto). Flute is a receptive character and seizes upon this tune to practise with growing confidence, volume, and pitch. Bottom's next infectious suggestion is his interpretation of the lion's part. This (with trombone roars) is taken up by the whole cast into a brief ensemble, "That would hang us, every mother's son". With the casting complete, a purposeful march (which has been forming inconspicuously in the orchestra from the beginning of the scene) is momentarily enjoyed and the cast disperse as earnestly as they came.

They assemble for the next rehearsal with a more business-like underlying rhythm. The first part of this scene is built on a pattern of the raising of difficulties, ensemble acknowledge-ment of them, and Bottom's solutions. The march from the previous scene introduces the rehearsal itself. The musical material of the play is a series of nicely balanced parodies and statements of the musically obvious. Flute's emerging indepen-dence is amusing to watch: he begins by singing his lines to Ex. 81, the only rhetorical style he knows, but is soon carried away with his own fluency and launches into a boldly sweep-ing tune at "Most briskly juvenal and eke most lovely Jew". At this point Bottom is "translated", but when he awakes after his period of enchantment it is to this cue, for which he was waiting an act ago. The *Pyramus and Thisby* play itself is a remarkable effort of sustained and wide-ranging parody: it is also tremendous fun, from the *Sprechstimme* of Wall, through *tenebroso* Victoriana and Gluck-style furies to the silly little flute tune that introduces each of Thisby's entries:

EX. 82

The most exciting aspect of Britten's *A Midsummer Night's Dream* is the way in which he has projected such formidably familiar material into a wholly musical and therefore wholly new dimension. So many moments in the opera—the opening fairy music for strings, the distraught Helena in Act I, Oberon waking Tytania, Thisby struggling into tune, and the solemn blessing of the palace at the end—are primarily musical experiences which exist quite independent of Shakespeare. There can be no doubt that Britten has created an entirely new drama from the material of the original, and the resulting opera constitutes a revelation, rather than a reinterpretation, of the play.

Chapter ten

Curlew River

Libretto by William Plomer from the play *Sumida-gawa* b
Jūrō Motomasa (1395–1431).
First performed Orford Church, June 1964.

CHARACTERS

THE ABBOT	Don Garrard, *bass*
THE FERRYMAN	{ John Shirley Quirk, *baritone* / Neil Howlett
THE TRAVELLER	Bryan Drake, *baritone*
THE MADWOMAN	{ Peter Pears, *tenor* / Robert Tear
THE SPIRIT OF THE BOY	{ Robert Carr / Bernard Morgan
HIS VOICE	{ Bruce Webb, *treble* / John Newton
THE CHORUS OF PILGRIMS	John Barrow
	Bernard Dickerson
	Brian Etheridge
	Edward Evanko
	John Kitchener
	Peter Leeming
	Philip May
	Nigel Rogers
THE PLAYERS	Richard Adeney, *flute*
	Neill Sanders, *horn*
	Cecil Aronowitz, *viola*
	Stuart Knussen, *double bass*
	Osian Ellis, *harp*
	James Blades, *percussion*
	Philip Ledger, *organ*

Production and Setting: Colin Graham
Costumes: Annena Stubbs
Movement instruction: Claude Chagrin
Music Directors: Benjamin Britten and Viola Tunnard

A company of Monks and their Abbot enter the church. The Abbot announces that they are to enact a mystery. Three of the Monks are ceremonially robed, as the Ferryman, the Traveller, and the Madwoman. The scene is set by a Fenland river in early medieval times.

THE PLAY: The Ferryman is preparing to cross the Curlew River. An important occasion is taking place on the far bank —the boat is full of pilgrims who are visiting a shrine there. The Traveller arrives and asks for a place in the boat. They hear the approaching Madwoman, who is singing crazily. She, too, asks for a place in the ferryboat; she is looking for her son who was seized by a stranger and taken eastwards. In spite of his habitual brusqueness, the Ferryman is moved by her quest and lets her embark.

While they are crossing the river the Ferryman tells the story of the shrine on the far bank. A year ago a barbaric stranger crossed the river, with a young boy whom he treated roughly. The boy was ill and the stranger left him to die. The boy told the river folk about his home in the west and asked to be buried by the path to the chapel, "Then, if travellers from my dear country pass this way, their shadows will fall on my grave." The river folk think he was a saint and claim miracles to have been worked at the grave.

They reach the other bank of the Curlew. The Madwoman discovers that she is the mother of the boy. In spite of her desolation at hearing of his death, she joins the pilgrims in prayer at her son's tomb. The boy's voice is heard and his spirit appears, to heal the mother of her madness.

The protagonists resume their Monks' habits and the Abbot makes a final address to the congregation before the procession of Monks forms again and departs singing the hymn to which they had entered.

Curlew River, a parable for Church performance, was first performed in Orford Church in June 1964. At first hearing it seemed to be a completely new operatic experience: but many of Britten's dramatic works have appeared to be new departures when, after the event, we can see them to be predictable from the course of development of the previous works. *Curlew River* can be seen as a successor to *Noye's Fludde*—in that the latter re-created the lay representation of religious drama in the late Middle Ages; *Curlew River* looks back to the earlier medieval liturgical drama, performed by the clergy, in church, the music very closely bound to the plainsong hymns which were incorporated in the drama. It can, however, also be seen as a logical culmination of chamber opera: the instruments are now endowed with such dramatic personality that the instrumentalists become participants in the drama (to an even greater extent in *The Burning Fiery Furnace*); the absence of a conductor is the natural sequel to this and the presence of certain random elements in the score—passages of which "no two performances are likely to be exactly the same" (Imogen Holst)—is made possible by the "chamber" interdependence of the singers and orchestra. The result—of the heritage of liturgical drama, the intimacy of chamber opera and the conductorless ensemble—is an unparalleled intensity in performance. It is interesting to find that this intensity was not only the result but equally the starting-point of the composition:

It was in Tokyo in January 1956 that I saw a Nō-drama for the first time; and I was lucky enough during my brief stay there to see two different performances of the same play—*Sumida-gawa*. The whole occasion made a tremendous impression upon me, the simple touching story, the economy of the style, the intense slowness of the action, the marvellous skill and control of the performers, the beautiful costumes, the mixture of chanting, speech, singing, which with the three instruments made up the strange music—it all offered a totally new 'operatic' experience.

There was no conductor—the instrumentalists sat on the stage, so did the chorus, and the chief characters made their entrance down a long ramp. The lighting was strictly non-theatrical. The cast was all male, the one female character wearing an exquisite mask which made no attempt to hide the male jowl beneath it.

. . . And so we came from *Sumida-gawa* to *Curlew River* and a church in the Fens, but with the same story and similar characters; and whereas in Tokyo the music was the ancient Japanese music jealously preserved by successive generations, here I have started the work with that wonderful plainsong hymn "Te lucis ante terminum" and from it the whole piece may be said to have grown. There is nothing specifically Japanese left in our Parable, but if we on the stage and you in the audience can achieve half the intensity and concentration of that original drama I shall be happy. (Britten in a programme note to the first production.)

And the prevailing musical process in *Curlew River* is intensification—of the melodic material. A technique common to early music both in England and Japan, and probably all the countries in between, is one known as heterophony: the simultaneous sounding of plain and decorated versions of the same tune. This primitive procedure, considerably developed in scope, is the basis of almost all the music in *Curlew River*. At its simplest it becomes a mechanical, unvarying texture:

G

EX. 83

When solo voices are involved freer rhythms are possible and allow a characterising phrase to develop:

EX. 84

The canonic potential of the technique is most often manifest in the Madwoman's music:

EX. 85

At the main climax, the prayer at the boy's tomb, there are two concurrent melodic paths each being decorated simultaneously. The process of heterophony as it is used in *Curlew River* varies from fugal texture ("Now let me show you where the boy is buried") to a blurred unison (the ceremonial robing of the protagonists); it proves to be both a rich source of new sonorities and a dramatic way of identifying the instruments with the vocal line. A prerequisite of the technique is a consistently melodic style. The opening of the opera gives some indication of how far the work is to depend on melody: it opens with the plainsong hymn "Te lucis ante terminum" sung while the Abbot, Monks, Acolytes and Instrumentalists process through the church to the acting area.

The plainsong is a naturalising influence on the Japanese story. Just as the congregational hymns in *Noye's Fludde* demonstrated both the lay nature of the original Miracle play and the amateur elements in the opera, so the procession of monks here affirms the ecclesiastical professionalism of the (medieval) performance that is being represented, as well as the ritualised style of the (twentieth-century) production which is actually taking place. The limited range of the hymn governs much of the material in the opera. Its intervals, mostly seconds and thirds, dominate the melodic lines of the Abbot and of the chorus of Monks whenever they are commenting on the action from their vocational standpoint: when they are taking part in the action their style is related more to that of the protagonists. Lines of the plainsong are quoted during the opera for various purposes: when in the Abbot's introduction he sings, "A sign was given of God's grace", he quotes the first line of "*Te lucis*" (repeated by the Chorus) to give the verbal phrase added significance. For this is the main theme of the opera: the purpose of suffering—the suffering of the boy and his mother—which gives rise to the miracle, the "sign of God's grace". The Madwoman is trying to escape from meaningless pain:

Where the nest of the curlew
Is not filled with snow,
Where the eyes of the lamb
Are untorn by the crow . . .
There let me go

When she sings this, the loss of her son appears to her to be in the same category. The opening phrase of the hymn is quoted again for the boy's dying prayer in the Ferryman's narrative, to underline this theme. But it is used purely musically when the Abbot sings "Beloved, attend to our mystery" at the end of his introduction, to give a cyclic feeling to the first part of this clearly symmetrical work.

There is a brief chorus during the introduction which contains a shape—repeated notes ending in a semitone drop (compare Ex. 88) which, with some variation in the extent and direction of the last interval, occurs frequently in the opera and is associated chiefly with the grief and suffering of the Madwoman. The words of this chorus indicate a subsidiary theme—the theme of the medieval performance that is being represented—"O pray for the souls of all that fall By the wayside, all alone". This idea is expanded later in the opera—

FERRYMAN: What is the use of tears?
            Whom can your weeping help?
            No, rather say a prayer
            That in the other world
            The soul of your child
            May rest in peace.

MADWOMAN: Cruel! Grief is too great,
            I cannot pray . . .

FERRYMAN : . . . Lady, remember,
            All of us here

May pray for your child:
But your prayer is best
To rejoice his young soul.

This interior theme is very much in the nature of a sermon
text as preached to the medieval congregation,* compared
with the vast implications of the main theme which *Curlew
River* shares with *Billy Budd*, *Lucretia*, and *The Little Sweep*.

The introduction is scored for chamber organ and drum.
The march which follows involves the remaining instruments
—flute, horn, viola, double bass, harp, and a group of five
small untuned drums. It consists of a metrical statement and
extension of "*Te lucis*" with a close canon at the octave and
a decorated version superimposed; the drums are played in
sequence up through their pitch range. It is ceremonial
music to accompany the robing of the protagonists. With the
opening of the innermost layer of the drama, personality
emerges for the first time.

And the Ferryman is a particularly forceful personality.
His characterising instrument is the horn (see Ex. 84) and to
a lesser extent the viola. This texture accompanies most of
his entries and can be compared with the wearing of masks
in this work—a potentially static act of characterisation that
is found to be amazingly flexible during the progress of the
opera. The two-note phrases of the horn derive from the
decoration of the march. In spite of the vigorous mood of his
exposition, the Ferryman's melodic line moves mainly in
seconds and thirds—the hymn is still controlling the material
very closely. The major/minor semitone ambivalence in the
horn and voice parts is typical of many passages in the work:
the chorus which has a central position in the Ferryman's
monologue (see Ex. 83) moves in this way. It is really another

---

* Not only are the instrumentalists incorporated in the action: the
audience is required to act the part of the medieval congregation, addressed
by the Abbot and instructed by the monks.

method of decoration, successive not simultaneous, of a simple outline—and the outline thus varied still contains no intervals greater than a third.

The approach of the Traveller reveals wider horizons and a less limited melodic style. His characterising instruments are the harp and double bass—sweeping arpeggios and a heavy trudging step:

EX. 86

—though he reverts to "*Te lucis*" for his prayer, "May God preserve wayfaring men". When he reaches the ferry the Traveller's instrumental voice holds a dialogue with the Ferryman's horn phrase some minutes before their verbal exchange.

The identification of the instruments with the characters is very powerful: it enables the flute entry (the same phrase as in Ex. 85) to announce unambiguously the entry of a new protagonist. This new instrumental voice is closely linked with the singing voice of the Madwoman—textually by the canon between them and dramatically because it represents an echo (although it precedes her phrases) implying her loneliness and expressing her agitation. Her first phrase

EX. 87

comes with a sense of shock after the restricted intervals of the previous music. It is later identified with the cry of the curlew. In the words of the riddle, through which her search for her son is interpreted, the Madwoman "cannot understand [their] cry": knowing this (a first time-audience could not), we can tell from these first notes that she cannot understand herself—she is mad. Her falling chromatic phrases are thrown into relief by the monotone of the Traveller at this point (who, incidentally, has a splendid seventeenth-century

effect: ♪ ♩♩♩♩♩♩♩ ♪,) and also by the monotone chat-
laugh - - - ing
tering of the chorus—

> We will delay the ferry-boat!
> We wish to see her.
> We wish to hear her singing.
> We will laugh at her
> Crazily singing.

The Chorus assumes its function as sympathetic commentator in the expressive passage "As she wanders raving, and all alone" and the ephemeral *scherzo* "Dew on the grass".*

The repeated note phrase which turns up or down by one degree (previously appearing as "O pray for the souls of all that fall" in the introduction and "in every season, in every weather" in the Ferryman's preamble) is now associated with

---

* A "score" of the highly controlled and formalised gestures is published along with the rehearsal score and the note for "Dew on the grass" runs as follows: "[The Madwoman] turns and throws herself on the ground, sweeping dew off imaginary grass blades with the palm of her right hand. (*N.B.* The hand must never touch the floor or illusion is destroyed.)" It seems a pity that such niceties should be advocated throughout when, in any church performance that allows the audience into the whole building, which means every performance so far given of this work, upwards of forty per cent of the audience are unable to see the Madwoman at this and several other points, let alone observe whether her hand brushes dew from the grass or dust from the floor. Necessarily this militates against the "intensity and concentration" the composer intended.

the Madwoman in her remarkable narrative aria, "Near the
Black mountains There I dwelt"

EX. 88

The expressive impact of this passage is achieved by the most
economical means: the final note of the figure. This note turns
up by a tone when the Madwoman recalls her life before the
tragedy. It is a colourless phrase, drained of emotion because
she cannot clearly remember life before her son was lost and
has no interest in it. By simply turning the last note down by
a tone instead of up,* we are shown how her world was
turned upside down by the event and that her grief is too
great to be expressed more artificially—in the literal sense.
The dropping interval becomes a semitone as the Madwoman broods not on her loss but on the fate of her son—
"seized as a slave, By a stranger, a foreigner"—and the last
remaining version, the rising semitone, depicts the dimension
of her search, and the remoteness of her son from all that is
familiar to her:

* The same interval, however, expresses the Spirits' consolation in the
miracle scene—the change of context accounts for the reversal of mood.

> They told me he was taken
> Eastward, eastward,
> Along the drovers' track
> East, east, east.

The portamento on the last important interval, of course, emphasises its direction and size. The repeated notes are transferred to the harp to accompany her weeping (over a reprise of the chorus "She wanders raving" to the words:

> A thousand leagues may sunder
> A mother and her son,
> But that would not diminish
> Her yearning for her child.)

The Ferryman mocks her, imitating her phrase—"So you come from the Black mountains!" His characteristic horn figure sounds particularly insensitive and blustering juxtaposed with the Madwoman's echoing flute. The transformation of his character is one of the minor miracles of the last scene; he shows a tendency to parody and bully her right up to the revelation of the Madwoman's identity. Indeed, he even drives her, though gently, into her miracle-producing prayer. It is this mockery that provokes the Madwoman into a temporary calm dignity: she expounds the riddle of the "famous traveller" (the harp links him with the Traveller in the opera):

EX. 89

Birds of the Fen-land, tho' you float or fly,   Wild birds, I   can-not   un-der-stand your cry,

Tell me— does the   one I   love   In—   this world still   live?

Here, the flute is not a haunting, tormenting echo to her words; it becomes the curlew's cry. The canonic relationship between the Madwoman's vocal line and the flute is no longer at the octave but at the tenth, indicating that the flute is now an independent voice. It remains, however, a closely related voice because "the one I love" in the riddle is, for the Madwoman, her son; and the flight of the curlew represents for her the boy's flight eastwards. All these ideas are developed in a beautiful passage for the Ferryman, Traveller, Chorus—and flute, very much a voice in the ensemble.

The Ferryman is moved by the unanimous appeals of the singers—"Ferryman, she begs of you To let her come aboard"—and hurries the Madwoman into the boat. Partly under the influence of his characteristic self-importance and partly to communicate the quite real danger of the crossing he issues appropriate warnings that culminate in the prayer "God have mercy upon us", which harks back to the plainsong. The sail is hoisted to a busy heterophonic instrumental interlude which melts into the slow glissandi of the river music as the boat is pushed off. The River Curlew is a potent factor in the drama. Unlike the sea in *Peter Grimes*, it does not give rise to tone pictures; rather, it shares with the Tiber in *Lucretia* the enacting of a metaphor. There are plenty of undertones of the Styx around the Curlew river—

> smoothly flowing
> Between the lands of East and West,
> Dividing person from person!

The Ferryman, too, is rude enough to be Charon! Crossing the river seems a decisive act for the Madwoman. She feels that she is near the end of her search, particularly after the riddle episode when she connects the flight of the curlews with the loss of her son. We are prepared for the miraculous appearance of the Spirit by the ironic words of the Chorus:

> Ah Ferryman, row your ferryboat!
> Bring nearer, nearer,

> Person to person,
> By chance or misfortune,
> Time, death or misfortune
> Divided asunder!

The idea that chance, misfortune, time or death do the dividing is easily transferred to the river itself. Its spiritual potency is manifest when, once across it, the Madwoman is granted a glimpse of the supernatural world. Structurally the river gives the opera a magnificent central section. The slow glissandi (which have magic connotations quite incidentally because, they are comparable with those in *The Dream*) provide a new background sonority for the important narration of the Ferryman's tale. As they are transferred from instrument to instrument they also reflect the changing emphasis of the story—double bass glissandi to accompany the description of the "stranger . . . arm'd with a sword and a cudgel"; the viola has them when the boy speaks, and the harp for his prayer and death. The impact of the boy's suffering on the Ferryman is significant—a process continued by the effect of the Madwoman's grief—and we can see it working fleetingly when the Ferryman interrupts his vigorous narrative for the aside "Poor child". The utterly damning phrase, "He was a man without a heart", and the tentative acceptance of the spiritual event—

> The river folk believe
> The boy was a saint.
> They take earth from his grave
> To heal their sickness.
> They report many cures.
> The river folk believe
> His spirit has been seen

—indicate in the Ferryman a more morally aware character than we witnessed on the west bank of the Curlew.

The Traveller and pilgrims disembark over a purposeful

descending ground bass which urges the necessarily slow action at this point towards the denouement. When only the Ferryman and the Madwoman are left in the boat his rough mockery returns and he again parodies Ex. 88—"You must be soft-hearted To weep at my story." He is also of course, mocking his own susceptibility. A classically tense passage of questioning follows; the impatience of the Ferryman is reflected in the drum accompaniment to his brusque replies, the restrained but mounting horror of the Madwoman by sustained chords with harp accents—building up from a single note for the double bass and harp to six-note chords for the whole orchestra. At her revelation, "He was the child Sought by this Madwoman", confusion ensues, culminating in the explosion of her grief, doubly violent after so much restraint, in her aria "O Curlew River, cruel Curlew!" This is the only place where the Madwoman explicitly identifies her son with the curlews: "Torn from the nest, my bird". This train of thought suggests a return to her earlier chromatic phrase— "Where the nest of the curlew is not filled with snow, Where the eyes of the lamb are untorn by the crow . . ." (subsequently her son is "the innocent lamb" and the stranger "The heathen crow"). Here, the original falling phrase is stated *fortissimo* in the orchestra, while the inversion of it appears in canon—

EX. 90

—which has the effect of affirming the universal wanton cruelty and the inevitability of suffering in the natural world which the Madwoman was still questioning on her first appearance—questioning and hoping to refute.

Her madness is not cured by her knowledge of the truth. The Madwoman is now deprived of what had become the purpose of her life—her search. Fragments from earlier episodes return: "You ask me Whither I, whither I go" (Ex. 85) is now "Where shall I, where shall I turn?"; the chorus "She wanders raving" becomes her bitter denunciation of the river and the birds whose cry she now understands only too well. The repeated notes of Ex. 88 reappear and the Ferryman obviously repents his parody of them when he sings "Who would have guess'd that The boy was her child?" Even the river chorus Ex. 83 has taken a fatalistic turn— "where the river for ever divides them".

A solemn passage expresses the transformation of the Ferryman's character: a combination of heterophonic technique and canon—

EX. 91

—an infinitely warm and comforting mood after the Madwoman's desolate reaction to the tragic narrative. But she is
not ready for spiritual consolation. Her thoughts still centre
on herself: a passage of almost motionless grief, "Hoping, I
wandered on", is another duet with the flute; the Madwoman develops the Ex. 88 figure by extending the last pair
of notes:

EX. 92

This represents the "chain on [her] soul"—her awareness of
the dead body of her son, its physical bond with her and its
continuing physical existence:

> In all this earth, no road
> Leads to my living son . . .
> I have come to a grave!
> Did I give birth to him
> To have him stolen
> And carried far, far away,
> Here to the Eastern Fens
> To end as dust by the road?
> O good people, open up the tomb
> That I may see again
> The shape of my child . . .

It is the Ferryman's function to mock and bully the Madwoman; here he imitates her Ex. 92 phrase gently: "What is
the use of tears?" At this point the bell begins tolling, presaging the musical climax and rendering predictable the spiritual
change in the Madwoman. There is at this point a most
lovely chorus—"The moon has risen"—one of the few
moments in the opera which is there for the sake of the beauty

of its sound rather than its function with regard to the plot or characterisation. In fact, it also prepares the first line of the hymn "*Custodes hominium*", which is the basis of the miracle scene. While the hymn is being sung by the Chorus, accompanied by the organ and decorated by the harp and viola, the Ferryman and the Traveller sing an ecstatic embellishment of the high bell notes. The mood of devotion is interrupted by a flute solo—curlew cries, which sound to the Madwoman disquietingly "like souls abandoned". She poses the riddle once more: "Tell me, does the one I love In this world still live?" and as if in answer the voice of the spirit of the boy is heard from the tomb. At this point there are at least five superimposed versions of the hymn, the spirit having the most conspicuous decoration, a delayed diminution of the theme. The spirit then appears, personified in a piccolo solo which relates his musical character closely to both the curlew phrase and the Ex. 88 figure. To the latter, the falling tone version, he bids his mother farewell. The Mother—now freed from her madness—sings "Amen", expanding not her son's prayer, nor his blessing, but, characteristically and inevitably (she is very human, and she is still a mother), the phrase in which he promises "we shall meet in heaven".

The climax is quickly over and the robing ceremonial follows instantly on the spirit's last "Amen". The Abbot's address closely balances his introduction. The chorus corresponding to "O pray for the souls of all that fall By the wayside" is sung to the rising semitone version of Ex. 88—"O praise our God that lifteth up The fallen, the lost, the least." The Abbot again concludes with the first line of "*Te lucis*"—"In hope, in peace, ends our mystery"—which is taken up as the performers process out.

This is a beautiful and very memorable work. Paradoxically, it has seemed to me even more beautiful and memorable after we have had its successor, *The Burning Fiery Furnace*. What Britten has done is to present us with a high point of sophistication in a series of dramatic works which bridge the gap between liturgical drama and *The Burning Fiery Furnace*, a series of developing intimacy, intensity, and single-minded unity between the librettist and the composer: only—the series itself happens not to have been written. *Curlew River* presupposes such a series, and in isolation it could seem less a refinement of (non-existent) predecessors than the arbitrary superimposition of "invented conventions" on material which might well have been less artificially presented. Of course, the "unwritten" series exists in the Nō-dramas which generated these parables. But with the composition of *The Burning Fiery Furnace* we have a native genre, and *Curlew River*, while remaining remarkably consistent within Britten's own operatic canon, falls into place as founder member.

Chapter eleven

The Burning Fiery Furnace

Libretto by William Plomer from the Book of Daniel.
First performed June 1966, in Orford Church.

CHARACTERS

THE ASTROLOGER (ABBOT)	Bryan Drake, *baritone*
NEBUCHADNEZZAR	{ Peter Pears, *tenor*
	{ Kenneth Macdonald
ANANIAS	{ John Shirley Quirk, *baritone*
	{ John Gibbs
MISAEL	{ Robert Tear, *tenor*
	{ Jack Irons
AZARIAS	{ Victor Godfrey, *bass*
	{ Edgar Boniface
THE ANGEL	Philip Wait, *treble*
ENTERTAINERS AND PAGES	Stephen Borton,
	Paul Copcutt
	Paul Davies
	Richard Jones
THE HERALD	Peter Leeming, *baritone*
THE CHORUS OF COURTIERS	Graham Allum
	Peter Lehmann Bedford
	Carl Duggan
	John Harrod
	William McKinney
	Malcolm Rivers
	Jacob Witkin
THE PLAYERS	Richard Adeney, *flute*
	Neill Sanders, *horn*
	Cecil Aronowitz, *viola*
	Keith Marjoram, *double bass*
	Roger Brenner, *alto trombone*
	Osian Ellis, *harp*
	James Blades, *percussion*
	Philip Ledger, *organ*

Production and Setting: Colin Graham
Costumes: Annena Stubbs
Movement instruction: Claude Chagrin
Music Directors: Benjamin Britten and Viola Tunnard

The Abbot introduces the play he and his Monks are to perform. The action of the play takes place in Babylon in the sixth century B.C. He relates that three young Israelites were brought to Babylon, having been bound by their fathers never in any way to betray their faith. The Abbot and five Monks are robed as an Astrologer, Nebuchadnezzar, a Herald, and Ananias, Misael and Azarias—the three young Israelites.

THE PLAY: A feast is held in honour of Ananias, Misael, and Azarias, who have been appointed to rule over three provinces of Babylon. They are given the Babylonian names of Shadrach, Meshach, and Abednego. When they refuse to eat and drink with the courtiers the Astrologer convinces Nebuchadnezzar that this is a calculated insult. The Herald announces the royal decree—that a great golden image of the Babylonian god Merodak is to be set up and:

> At what time ye hear the sound of the cornet,
> Flute, harp, sackbut, psaltery, dulcimer
> And all kinds of music
> Ye fall down and worship the image of gold.
> Whose falleth not down and worshipeth
> Shall be cast into the midst
> Of a burning fiery furnace.

The musicians circulate in procession and return to the acting area. The image of Merodak has been set up. The Babylonians sing a hymn to Merodak:

> Gold is our God,
> Fall down and worship it.

The Astrologer repeatedly tells Nebuchadnezzar that Shadrach, Meshach, and Abednego will not worship the image; eventually Nebuchadnezzar interrogates them and hearing their refusal to acknowledge Merodak he has the furnace prepared for their execution.

The three Israelites are cast into the furnace, and are seen standing unhurt in the fire with a fourth figure among them. With this angel, they sing (the *Benedicite*) in praise of their God.

Nebuchadnezzar summons them to come out of the furnace and they reappear quite untouched by the fire. Nebuchadnezzar repudiates his Astrologer and is converted to the God of Shadrach, Meshach, and Abednego, "Who hath sent his angel And delivered them who put their trust in him." The protagonists resume their Monks' habits and the Abbot makes a final address to the congregation before the procession re-forms and departs singing the hymn to which the cast had entered.

The Burning Fiery Furnace is Britten's second parable for church performance and it seems at this point in time to be essentially a sequel. It is hard to imagine that it could, accidentally, have been the first of the genre: "*The Burning Fiery Furnace* develops the convention invented by Benjamin Britten for *Curlew River*" (William Plomer, in a programme note to the first production). To what extent can one invent a convention? Particularly in opera, "convention" implies some technique or artifice understood by the audience—and something which would not be fully understood unless it had become "conventional". Conventions evolve.*

Much of the success of *Curlew River* lies in the extent to which the limiting and stylised procedure (which is what Plomer calls "the convention") arises naturally from the material of the drama. Three reactions are, I think, possible to *Curlew River*: that it is an entirely arbitrary novelty; that it is so redolent of dramatic traditions native to both this country and Japan that it can be seen as a culmination of them rather than a new departure; that the form is the only satisfactory one in which to express this particular story. When we come to *The Burning Fiery Furnace* there is no inevitability in the relationship between form and subject. *The Furnace* has a diffuse plot (dealing not with individual grief but conflicting races, and not with an interior spiritual miracle but with spectacular paganism) which is crammed into the forms of *Curlew River*. It is at this point that these forms start to become

* J. D. S. Pendlebury, in *Ancient Crete*, points out that no Cretan potter turned over in bed and informed his wife, "From now on it'll be Late Minoan III"; and while, on the other hand, Gluck informed a great number of people that from 1767 overtures were to become relevant to the dramas they introduced, this never became conventional in his lifetime.

conventions. Nevertheless, *The Burning Fiery Furnace* is a less esoteric experience than *Curlew River*. The musical material is more varied, there is more polyphony, more spectacle, more entertainment (in *Curlew River* the Madwoman had to "entertain" the Ferryman and his passengers with her singing, which was no entertainment for the audience. In *The Furnace* both the Babylonian and the twentieth-century audiences are entertained by the diversion during the feast)—there is more action in the score and on the stage.

The Burning Fiery Furnace also seems less remote because the story of Shadrach, Meshach, and Abednego is a generally familiar one which involves the audience—or at least the medieval congregation they are representing—in identification with the three young men. It is from their point of view that we see the country of their captivity: the opera is about exotic Babylon rather than stateless Judah. In consequence it is a highly coloured picture of the "outlandish" nation that dominates the opera. "To them we are the foreigners", one faction among the prejudiced courtiers perceives, and it is this view thich dictates the colouring and musical diction of the opera. There are three great spectacles in the opera—the feast, the image of Merodak, and the furnace. And something of the richness of sounds which expresses these is implicit from the first notes of the opera.

The plainsong, "*Salus aeterna*", with which the work opens, indicates a potential intervalic range far wider than "*Te lucis*", which opened *Curlew River*—it spans a minor seventh instead of a fourth and outlines chordal shapes. This is important to the use of this material in the opera—unlike *Curlew River* the music does not expand physically from the limited intervals of the plainsong. The Abbot's introduction is already wide-ranging, freely derived from "*Salus aeterna*". But in conjunction with the plainsong his introduction establishes in the first ten bars a sufficiently significant style for the Jewish/Christian norm of the opera that the phrase

EX. 93

stands out as a colourful signpost to the foreign element which is to be fully explored. We are not only made aware of its foreignness: before the end of the introduction our view of Babylon is morally prejudged when Ex. 93 is used for the words "an evil man". The other distinctive phrase of the Abbot's introduction is

EX. 94

which is developed from a phrase of the plainsong—at "*Mox tua spontanea*"—with the jagged interval of the minor ninth created by transposing one note down an octave. This phrase expresses the identity of the three young men throughout the opera—closely associating them with the plainsong and therefore the audience, medieval and twentieth-century; it also conveys something of their uncomfortable non-conformity as seen by the Babylonians. It is transferred to the Monks when they utter the interior theme of the drama—the theme of the medieval instruction—

> God give us all
> The strength to stand
> Against the burning,
> Murderous world!

The theme of the whole drama is a quality of character, "steadfastness"—which the three young men possess and Nebuchadnezzar conspicuously lacks, even in his conversion.

The ceremonial robing is carried on during a heterophonic variation of *"Salus aeterna"*—more complex than the corresponding number in *Curlew River*, with a cadenza-like harp line which picks out and extends the intervals of a third in the plainsong. The herald announces the feast in honour of the three young men. The trombone, loosely decorating the vocal line, is full of "Babylon" arpeggios, and when Ananias, Misael and Azarias acknowledge the invitation the horn recalls Ex. 94.

In the musical language of Babylon individual words are set to marked and precise rhythms which contrast with the plainsong, the Abbot's and the Jewish music. In particular we have ♩ ♪ ♪♩ ♪♩ and ♪ ♪♩ and the renaming of

Neb - u - chad-nezz-ar   Bab - y - lon

the three young men as ♩ ♪ ♩ ♪ ⁊ ♪ ♪♪♪♪

'Shad-rach,   Me-shach,   Ab - ed - ne - go'

(*The Burning Fiery Furnace* is based on a style of thematically significant recitative rather than the essentially lyrical diction in *Curlew River*—this is as much a result of the compression and limitation of the incidents as it is a method of characterising the verbally eloquent public life of Babylon. The Jewish music is close to the overall style of *Curlew River*, without ever having sufficient room for expansion to be lyrical. It is governed by the intervals of the plainsong, it is a-metric, and most of the heterophony in the opera—for example, their big central soliloquy, "We do not lack enemies"—occurs in their music. It is very direct and economical: by the end of that soliloquy the three young men are identified in a single chord. The Babylonian music is purposely less refined—its primitive ethos is demonstrated in its rhythmic and generally metrical style, and it is never condensed as in the example of the single chord; it takes place in spectacular contexts—the herald's two proclamations, the feasting, the hymn to Merodak, and above all the processional march. It is melodically short-winded rather than compressed. The courtiers either chatter, or imitate instrumental flourishes.)

Two styles of chorus ensue and the recitative idiom is carried through into "O joyful occasion The King gives a feast"—a spontaneous chorus we would have called "gossip type" in *Peter Grimes*. (The Babylonians are great gossips and have plenty of these self-revealing choruses without ever quite revealing enough of themselves for the purposes of characterisation. We never know their real attitude to their religion— we never know the Astrologer's—and we can only suspect, not demonstrate, that Nebuchadnezzar is the only spiritually aware Babylonian). For the arrival of Nebuchadnezzar, a festive march with heterophonic flourishes for flute, harp and horn is transferred to the chorus, imposing instrumental function and rhythm on the voices. Probably we are meant to identify not a little with the Babylonians, too. Dramatically they are an average enough civilisation: it is the musical scheme of the drama and the force of continuing Christianity implied in the "convention" (above all, in the use of plainsong) that commits us to the three young men.

Nebuchadnezzar is perhaps the most colourful convert in the Old Testament. In this scene we see him as a thriving and popular ruler. He is intuitively—or under divine guidance—drawn to the Jewish exiles (and discerning enough to have turned the sack of Jerusalem into a compulsory "brain-drain"). At the same time he is deeply dependent on the Astrologer: his opening recitative is accompanied by references to Ex. 93 and Ex. 94 but is derived from the intervals of

EX. 95

—a phrase which is associated with the pagan magic of the
Astrologer and expresses another aspect of exotic Babylon.
The three young men are colourless in comparison—their
first ensemble, based on Ex. 94, is typical of their unanimity
of character and the uninteresting rightness of everything
they do, whether it is replying with exaggerated courtesy to
Nebuchadnezzar's kingly hospitality or making their avowal
of steadfastness which gets them into the furnace. There is
no attempt at idiosyncratic characterisation—their role as
audience representative is too important, and they have
also to portray the loneliness and persecution of a whole
race.

The entertainment by the acolytes is refreshingly thin and
active music after the "wallowing in excessive feast":

EX. 96

The clarity of the tunes and the transparent structure is as
satisfying as all of Britten's music for children. In such a

tightly packed work there is no room for a mere interlude. The episode has a dramatic function apart from adding an extra layer to the dimensionally rich feast scene—the carefree detachment of the boys highlights both the hedonistic Babylonians and the conscience-wracked Jews. The "waters of Babylon" are a suggested comparison with two opposites, both the "King's precious wine" and the "sevenfold heat Of the burning fiery furnace". The entertainment represents innocence set against civilisation—the dark civilisation and the enlightened.

When the three young men refuse to join in the feast, another relationship is developed: that between Nebuchadnezzar and his Astrologer. Nothing could be more genuinely gracious than Nebuchadnezzar gently pressing Shadrach, Meshach, and Abednego to partake:

Ex. 97

(The whole dialogue takes place over an inversion on the viola of their excuse, "We are very small eaters": in its rising form it becomes identified with "the sacred laws of Israel".) The Astrologer was quick to draw attention to their abstinence —to Ex. 94 he rudely sings:

> There may be in your country
> Bad behaviour at table,
> But here in Babylon
> Our guests do not insult us.

When the King is faced with the nonconformity of his protégés the Astrologer reminds him of the magic powers at issue, in Ex. 95:

> I warned you
> The stars were against you.
> This rash innovation,
> Invasion of immigrants,
> Puts Babylon in danger.

The moral judgements of this opera are pre-empted by virtue of the Abbot's words in the Prologue. It is not, otherwise, easy to make out a case for the Astrologer being the villain of the drama: he probably is "always faithful" to Nebuchadnezzar and is certainly "always faithful to [his] duty" if we regard that duty as promoting the worship of Merodak in whom the Astrologer may well sincerely believe. On the other side we can show that he is a graceless character musically, he is rude and wilfully inaccurate ("invasion of immigrants" is an emotive phrase, but it has nothing to do with the captivity of Judah), and both at the feast and before the image of Merodak it is he who points out the defaulting Jews of whom he is professionally jealous. His power over Nebuchadnezzar is indisputable. At the mention of the stars, Nebuchadnezzar launches into an arioso of panic and isolation:

EX. 98

It is the nearest he comes to an aria in the opera. (I think we miss the revelations of introspective arias in the characterisation of both Nebuchadnezzar and the Astrologer. The ambiguities in both their characters could have been resolved in one soliloquy each.) We can compare the panic with that which seizes Vere, his Scylla and Charybdis, when he realises the trial he has set in motion will condemn not Billy but himself; he is a very similarly impetuous man. And the isolation with Gloriana in her dilemma over Essex's death. The crises of authority are shown, in Britten's operas, to be just as painful as the physical punishment with which they are usually associated. Nebuchadnezzar, his "best intentions" frustrated, is a baffled barbarian—the antithesis of the steadfast man. His courtiers do not share his indecision. Some of them align themselves with the Astrologer, in Babylonian intervals (see Ex. 93); others in a flowing phrase derived from Ex. 98 present a less prejudiced point of view:

> He is jealous,
> The young men are harmless . . .
> To them we are the foreigners!

The pagan and Christian powers confront each other when the Astrologer's (off-stage) ominous mention of "Merodak" is immediately followed by a return (on the horn) of the opening of the plainsong: Shadrach, Meshach, and Abednego are left alone in physical and ideological isolation. They cling vocally to the symbol of their faith—between changing versions of the opening phrase of "*Salus aeterna*" they discuss their plight in phrases which use only the notes of the preceding variation of the plainsong:

EX. 99

They are only released from this tightly organised form when they sing, to the *Salus aeterna* phrase, "What we are we remain" —and the plainsong melody is completed with more flowing embellishment, interrupted three times by the line "Lord, help us in our loneliness" with which this detailed exploration of the hymn ends.

The Herald, in a similar passage to the opening of the drama, announces the setting-up of the image of Merodak, and the required worship. The agitation of the three young men is indicated in their Ex. 94 phrase on the harp and the $^7_3\sharp$ chord, which was finally associated with "Lord, help us in our loneliness" in the previous ensemble, on the organ. This chord is used throughout their short hymn—"Blessed art Thou, O Lord God of our fathers"—and at the same time in the orchestra the phrases of the processional march are assembled.

The procession of the musicians follows. It is interesting to

see how this incident is apparently dictated by the plot and
language of the original story, while at the same time what
is happening—the involvement of the orchestra in the physical
action of the drama—is something towards which each of
Britten's chamber operas has been tending. The phrases
which are put together to make the march are stated singly
during the prayer of the three young men mentioned above.
The Babylonian drum has a five-bar repeated pattern occa-
sionally combined with or relieved by the small cymbals. The
other instruments add their individual themes in turn, without any extensions or development: the horn has a leaping,
dotted phrase with plenty of Babylonian fourths, but essentially decorating a rising major chord which turns in by a
semitone. The trombone embellishes the same shape with
chromatic detail, a tone lower. The viola has wide arpeggios
on D and E♭ which combine with, on their first appearance,
an intense flute theme of four chromatically descending notes;
there is a busy, small-compassed phrase for the glockenspiel,
concerned with a rising major chord which turns up by a tone,
and a scale-wise tune for the Little Harp, filling in various
intervals of a fifth. These are combined cumulatively in an
orgy of sound. As the image of Merodak is raised the
themes merge into sweeping glissandi and the chorus joins in
with phrases based on a rising fourth or fifth, turning down or
up by a semitone—phrases which are literally a gross simplifi-
cation of the various strands of the march. The hymn to
Merodak arises out of the march, dramatically and thematically—a grovelling, barbaric, and superbly pagan utterance:

EX. 100

Me-ro - - dak!   Lord - of cre-a-tion,   We bow___down be-fore you,

A - dore you,   Im-plore you

Nebuchadnezzar and the Astrologer exhort the people to a louder demonstration and in between *fortissimo* unanimous cries of "Merodak!" (chorded in superimposed fourths derived from Ex. 95) and over a tense organ trill, the Astrologer twice cautiously draws Nebuchadnezzar's attention to the defaulting Jews. Nebuchadnezzar replies:

> Must you disturb me while I pray?
> Let me alone! . . .
> Must you bring complainings at this time?
> Go away!

Nebuchadnezzar's reluctance is striking. He is possibly the only sincere worshipper before the image of Merodak and, impulsive and enthusiastic, he is not interested in the disobedience of the Jews. The third time the Astrologer speaks he mentions not their disobedience but their impiety—

> Sir, they serve not your God,
> Nor worship the image
> You have set up

—and this rouses the king to send for them, when he puts his and their predicaments with undeniable though inflexible fairness. Nebuchadnezzar is not yet enraged; that he has to repeat much of the Herald's music, when he reminds the three young men of his decree, gives the semblance of a trial to his interrogation.

The three young men reply with tranquil acceptance in the opening phrase of "*Salus aeterna*" and their characteristic $^7_3\sharp$ chord. Because the musical organisation of the Parables is so compressed, characters who repeat the words of others almost always repeat their notes, too—so, without a hint of the mocking parody that the Ferryman exercises over the Madwoman in *Curlew River*, Shadrach, Meshach, and Abednego sing "Nor worship the image of gold Which you have set up, in Babylon the Great" to the theme of the hymn to

Merodak. (Their perpetual discreet politeness indicates that this is a "conventional" parody, not a mocking one.) It does, however, provoke Nebuchadnezzar into making his first unprompted decision in the opera:

EX. 101

This becomes a chorus, "See them all go up in smoke", with the theme divided between and developed by the trombone (bar 1) and the horn and organ (bar 2), and a piccolo phrase which extends the "Babylon" arpeggio. At the climax of this movement, "the flames open and the Three are seen standing unhurt with a radiant figure beside them". The full body of sound gives way to the unaccompanied *Benedicite* which, with interruptions, continues until the end of the drama:

EX. 102

Nebuchadnezzer is quick to perceive that a miracle has ocurred (or is it just that the drama is being enacted in such a small time-scale?) and his conversion is already manifest when he sings the *Salus aeterna* phrase for "And the form of the fourth Is like the Son of God." When the three young men come out of the furnace he inspects them with immense caution, however, while the double bass and viola remind him

H

of the "sevenfold heat" which has not even scorched their garments.

Nebuchadnezzar rejects the Astrologer with more prejudice than he showed in confronting the three young men with their default. The imperfections in Nebuchadnezzar's character—his irrational enthusiams and the injustice that repeatedly results from them—are nowhere more clearly shown than in this scene between the King and his sage. Ex. 95 is everywhere dominant, on the flute and harp and in the voice lines.

The *Benedicite* continues, with Nebuchadnezzar aligned with the three young men and the courtiers joining in antiphonally. The angel phrase continues to float above the whole. It is a quiet climax, very simple musically: the miracle is all. It is remarkable that both Parables court the opportunity of portraying miracles in music and both deal with the visions in a style so self-effacing at this point as to throw all the emphasis on to the verbal or visual account of the supernatural. Britten belongs (like Shakespeare, Dickens, Bach, Schumann) among artists who are concerned to portray human suffering, and even martyrdom, rather than among the interpreters of the Beatific Vision (Handel, Haydn, Traherne, Herbert, and C. S. Lewis). It leads directly into the robing music and the Abbot's epilogue which indicates musically as well as verbally that "Over that great city, Babylon . . . A new light shines"—Babylon is sung for the first time without its pagan-characterising motif; it spans instead a minor seventh—the compass of the plainsong. "A new light" is sung to the rising fourths of Ex. 96—it has literally taken the place of the Astrologer's rule. The Abbot naturally uses Ex. 101 for his development of the interior theme:

Friends, remember!
Gold is tried in the fire,

And the mettle of man
In the furnace of humiliation.

The chorus complete this to Ex. 94—

God give us all
The strength to walk
Safe in the burning furnace
Of this murderous world.

And because the plainsong has been more dramatically integrated in this work than it was in *Curlew River*, it is with a
sense of concluding the inner drama, the Nebuchadnezzar
story, rather than the completion of a formal frame, that the
Monks take up *Salus aeterna* for their final procession.

Chapter twelve

Britten and Opera

Throughout the canon of eleven operas discussed in this book runs the fact, paradox or truism, of their apparent variety and their internal predictability. Their variety we can dispose of in a sentence: they are immensely individual operas. Their predictability, or rather the predictability of Britten's approach to the different dramas, requires amplification. Britten's approach to the music, to the libretto and to the drama itself is sufficiently consistent to be characteristic, and it is this approach—always having in mind the wide context in which it is operating—which I shall try to define and illustrate in this chapter.

The most characteristic aspect of Britten's approach to the music is his concern to express drama in terms of sheer physical sound. This is a very sensuous approach to audience manipulation, the equivalent of rhetoric. We have a series of highly coloured dramas, a character depicted in a single sonority or timbre; events, even, conveyed in a succession of themeless sounds. But Britten's expression of drama through sonorities is a more economical process than the previous sentence implies. There is a constant tendency throughout the operas to refine orchestral forces and expose chamber groups, to communicate the characteristic qualities of voices and instruments as individually as possible, a technique which tends towards the utmost precision of communication and unambiguous presentation of the essential colour of the drama.

The thinness of orchestral sound in some of the full operas is perhaps surprising until we regard it in this light—as relevant communication. There are, for example, numerous occasions in *Billy Budd* where a couple of woodwind instruments are all that is used to introduce significant material—as at the opening of the first scene. Or even one—the saxophone solo in the Novice's flogging scene. Or a single family of instruments—the trumpet and trombone call to vigilance that breaks up the scene in Vere's cabin in Act I, Scene 2; and the trombones plus tuba which have the "hanging from the yard-arm" phrase at Billy's execution. Or a temporarily created family—the oboes and muted trumpets when the Novice tries to bribe Billy. The culmination of the eloquence of sonority, when Vere tells Billy the verdict of death, is only possible when in the whole of the opera the speaking quality of sounds is exposed. In the chamber operas we find the creation of many smaller ensembles from the already limited forces. There are, as in the full operas, many moments when the instrumental texture is carried on by one instrument. In *Lucretia* it is initially the flute alone which depicts the Tiber, the cor anglais which sings a duet with the doomed Lucretia; a family of instruments to be explored here is the bass, tenor, and side drums, notably in Tarquinius's stealthy approach to Lucretia's bed (a passage from which we could trace the very vital and individual use made of drums in the Parables), and the oboe and bassoon in octaves in Lucretia's wreath-making song.

During the whole series of operas, Britten increasingly uses instruments to express not just colour—anonymous, if exciting or beautiful timbre—but character and personality. The tensions and drama here are created by balancing the natural and universal character of the instrument with the unique and idiosyncratic character of the protagonist with which it is identified. The celesta, for example, is an intrinsically chilling and supernatural sound. When it is heard briefly at the death of the second apprentice in *Peter Grimes* it evokes little more than this inevitable other-worldliness. In *The Turn of the Screw*, by contrast, it plays a much bigger part, and while remaining supernatural in its impact it also cxprcsscs, through its context and association with Quint, a positively evil aura. In *A Midsummer Night's Dream* it has again a prominent role. Here, the style of the music is quite different from the arpeggio layout of the passage in *Peter Grimes* and many of its appearances in *The Screw*. It brings its supernatural colouring to the spell music, but in the context of this drama and in association with Oberon it conveys the detached amorality of his passionless power. The flute in *Curlew River* is a very idiosyncratic one: it is half identified with the Madwoman (it is her "voice" before we hear her sing) and half independent of her (indeed, positively eluding her when it becomes the cry of the curlews). The whole drama is condensed into the relationship between the Madwoman's voice and the flute: the instrument is both the cause and the expression of her madness. In *Noye's Fludde* the sonorities not only express but aurally depict the drama. The concluding Addison hymn is a conglomeration of sounds where the individual lines are so sharply, even crudely, coloured that they remain separate, not homogenous, and thus demonstrate a coming together of a great many centuries of faith from the mythical Noye through our own Middle Ages, Tallis, Addison, to the present —rather than a conclusion in any one of these periods which would limit the implications of the expression of faith.

Britten's pursuit of significant sound is not restricted to the orchestra. The Choruses are also to be listened to from this point of view. All the Choruses in Britten's operas are involved in the drama—acting Choruses. In *Peter Grimes*, *Billy Budd*, *Noye*, and *The Burning Fiery Furnace* they have real personality and intensify rather than relieve the protagonists' scenes. In *Grimes* and *Budd* particularly their collective character is vital to the progress of the plot; in these operas they are less a part of the background picture than an accumulation of individuals. In *Billy Budd* even their background function is broken down into a series of definitions in the structure of the sea-fight scene: the Chorus has a part to act whether it is as potential mutineers or efficient seamen. *Curlew River*, because of its "convention", appears to have some choruses which comment on the action. But although it is not the pilgrims talking when the Chorus sings

> Or will they also laugh at her
> As she wanders raving, and all alone?

it is the Monks, impersonating the pilgrims, who are indeed acting, and in this sense the Chorus is a dramatically involved one. *The Furnace* is so packed with action and incident that there is no room even for this half-detachment: the Monks become Nebuchadnezzar's courtiers for the duration of the inner drama, and sing accordingly. *Gloriana* is a special case: the Chorus does comment, in the public scenes, but it is not a simple assembly of individuals like the people of the Borough in *Peter Grimes*; in *Gloriana* it represents the whole nation and expresses its reactions spontaneously enough if we remember the extra dimension it involves.

As a result (of the dramatic involvement of the Chorus), the sounds we hear from the Choruses are basically representational ones. Even the big fugal scenes in *Grimes* have a dramatic cause for the given texture: the confusion and concern at the approaching storm is portrayed quite naturally (as well as formally) in the ensemble "Look out for squalls!" in Act I; the big chorus movement, "Grimes is at his exercise", in the second act, conveys in terms of sound the swift interchange of ideas and the spreading into unanimity of the key thought. The working songs of the men in *Billy Budd* are written in a way that condenses much of the drama into the differences between the successive versions: the suppressed tensions in "O heave" in the first scene of Act I are expressed in the fleeting mutiny attempt at the end of the opera. The potential tensions are indicated when to the flowing, monotonous first statement of the Chorus is added the theme a major third higher, first in canon then simultaneously. This is the potential rebellion which reaches its frustrated, poignant climax not in the violent diminution of the theme which is sung during the brief mutiny episode but in the *largamente* transformation of it as the men are subdued and dispersed: the climax of the potential drama in the first-act chorus is frustration, not rebellion—this is what the opera is about. The fact that in the last act it is a wordless chorus concentrates our attention on the actual sound of the drama.

Another characteristic of Britten's approach to the music is his tendency to express drama in lyrical terms. This is really the other side of the sonority coin—it is at these moments not the sound of massed or selected choral or instrumental forces but of a single voice, which is used so that it is subservient to neither the words nor the external action. Britten's approach to opera is essentially lyrical and there is a tendency throughout the operas to tackle not only characterisation but situations and incidents—not in overtly "dramatic" music but in melody. There are, significantly, many characters in the operas which are created not just in aria but in song—Billy, Essex (and Cecil and Raleigh), Miles, and Flute. And many others, notably Quint, Grimes, Albert Herring, and Oberon, who are revealed almost exclusively in closed solo numbers rather than in action, dialogue or recitative. It becomes, for Grimes, Herring, and perhaps Miles, a paradox that these characters reveal in song and aria their true natures which could not be deduced from their actions: Quint and Essex, on the other hand, used closed lyrical forms to communicate a misleading impression of their characters (they both attempt seduction in song, and both fail).

But the lyricism throughout Britten's operas has a wider function than characterisation: complex situations are conveyed to the audience in surprisingly lyrical contexts. Here are five of them. The actual rape of Lucretia is led up to in a duet and formalised in an ensemble which is the second of three variations of a particularly expansive "motto melody". The confrontation of Lucretia and Collatinus in the last scene is not argued but stated (in terms of melody—the cor anglais solo): after recollected fragments of earlier melodies, Lucretia has the final variation of the motto melody, then she and Collatinus share a solemn *andante* which disintegrates as she stabs herself. In the last scene of *The Screw*, the tense questioning and verbal fencing is communicated in the freshest of melodic lines—"Dearest Miles, I love to be with you, what else should I stay for?" In the trial scene in *Billy Budd* the officers reach their verdict in a long melody which emerges from the trio, passing from one voice to another, in between unison statements of "We've no choice". Finally, *The Little Sweep* has a comparatively extended ensemble movement, continuously lyrical—"O why do you weep through the working day?"—to represent a conversation.

What has the lyrical approach added to these five events? In the two examples from *Lucretia* it prevents the physical violence from dominating the episodes and allows the music to express the artistic truth of the incidents: the recurrence of the "motto melody" at both climaxes could indicate either the apparent cause of the tragic events—Junius's jealousy which is described in the first appearance of the motto melody, or, by its very repetition, and therefore inevitability, it could imply "fate" as being the real cause of the tragedy—whatever this would mean. In *The Screw* the relevant dramatic process is the passacaglia, but this generates a fluently lyrical superstructure to demonstrate the passionate possessiveness of the Governess and the dilemma which for Miles has been expressed throughout the opera as song, or rather songs—his own "Malo" and Quint's "On the paths, in the woods". The trial scene in *Billy Budd* is a remarkable movement from any aspect. For our purposes here, the lyrical treatment of the officers' deliberations is used partly to indicate the actual progress of the discussion: the unanimity

of their opinions here (in contrast to their immediate reactions to Claggart's death) is shown when each adds corro-
borative arguments to complete the melodic line:

> FIRST LIEUTENANT: Poor fellow, who could save him?
> LIEUTENANT RATCLIFFE: Ay! there's nought to discuss.
> SAILING MASTER: Ay! he must swing.
> ALL: We've no choice.
> FIRST LIEUTENANT: There's the Mutiny Act.
> LIEUTENANT RATCLIFFE: There are the King's Regula-
> tions.
> SAILING MASTER: There are the Articles of War.
> ALL: We've no choice.
> FIRST LIEUTENANT: Claggart I never liked . . .
> SAILING MASTER: Claggart, no one liked Claggart . . .
> LIEUTENANT RATCLIFFE: Claggart was hard on them
> all . . .

The proliferation of thoughts is also contrasted with the
summing up—"We've no choice". The conversation in *The
Little Sweep* is one that could never have taken place in the
dialogue and the deliberately formal treatment of the words
enables them to be stated by the children—the thoughts
expressed are far too sophisticated philosophically to be
uttered in realistic conversation, yet once they are used as the
basis of a closed number they are expressible in the simplest
musical diction which for these protagonists is song.

The third aspect of Britten's approach to the music I shall
illustrate is his expression of drama through form. Form in
opera has to do with the two processes, separateness and continuity. They are actually a single factor, each being a
matter of degree: continuity may be a question of themes,
keys, sonorities or verbal or musical thought; separateness
may exist within this, as an episode. Separateness comes about
through contrasted means of expression which for the most

part of the history of opera have been differentiated as recitative and aria. Such a dichotomy from the point of view of style is no longer viable, but the contrasted functions remain: continuity is for the action of the drama (traditionally recitative) and separateness for the musical exploration of the emotional repercussions (traditionally aria).

Since Britten is particularly concerned with characterisation—and some of his operas consist of characterisation and little else: *Grimes, Gloriana, The Screw, Curlew River*, for example—he is inevitably concerned with the emotional exploration traditionally conducted in aria and in separated numbers. This is why there are in his operas a lot of separate numbers which are, in fact, arias for Grimes, Gloriana, Quint, and the Madwoman. There are also whole scenes, however, for these protagonists which are solely concerned with displaying the one character but in a style and formal process far removed from the traditionally lyrical definition of aria: they are arias in function rather than in form. And they are not usually separated from the continuous action.

In *Peter Grimes*, Interlude IV and the whole of Act II, Scene 2, are a complete movement. In spite of some quite definite action (including the death of the boy) the whole expanse of music has the function of an aria, and the dramatic conflict of reality and dreams in the mind of Peter Grimes is organised as relevantly in the music as the key and subject groups of eighteenth-century sonatas. "Reality" is dealt with at length in the passacaglia, the bass of which is Grimes's acceptance of himself, the notes to which he sang "[so be it, and] God have mercy upon me". Fragments of the passacaglia continue into the scene to interrupt real enough action as Grimes and his apprentice prepare to go fishing. Reality not only interposes in the scene but is also integrated into the new material—Grimes's intitial "Go there" decorates a falling twelfth (the viola theme of the passacaglia decorates a falling fifth) and ends with three characteristic notes from the viola theme. The central section of the scene is the dream and here the music departs completely from the passacaglia material (and reality). It has its own thematic unity: in the outer *Lento* section the conspicuous phrase of a rising major sixth turning inwards at the words "[in dreams I've built myself some] kindlier home" and "[where there'll be no more fear and] no more storm"—this visionary, aspiring interval is incorporated mechanically into the accompaniment of the middle (*Adagio*) section which builds upon the verbal and musical suggestions of the *Lento* bars. When the music returns to the *Lento* material, "But dreaming builds what dreaming can disown", the fact that Grimes's dreams are destroyed within this dream section shows that it is not only in reality that Grimes cannot achieve his ideal but also in the (for him) greater reality of his dreams:

> I hear those voices that will not be drowned
> Calling, there is no stone
> In earth's thickness to make a home,
> That you can build with and remain alone.

Significantly, reality (and the passacaglia material) returns not with Hobson's drum but with what Grimes—confused now about what is true and what appears to be happening—deludedly thinks is the cause of the procession; he says to the boy:

> You've been talking!
> You and that bitch were gossiping!
> What lies have you been telling?

Reality (the last appearance of the passacaglia bass) inevitably accompanies Balstrode's exit down the cliff, in pursuit of the truth. The musical structure of this scene illuminates the whole dramatic predicament of Grimes. It is the heart of the drama. It can also be defined as an aria.

It is owing to the character-based drama which is typical of Britten's operas that these scenes are "separate" in function and "continuous" in structure. They do not, in the spirit of Gluck's criticisms of aria form, hold up the action; instead, the drama at that point happens to be going on in Grimes's mind. However, there are certainly moments in *Peter Grimes* and other operas which do go against the spirit of Gluck's operatic ideal (which is neither a criticism of Britten nor of Gluck, but simply a reminder that there are always these two approaches to drama in music).* In all the operas—except *Billy Budd, The Screw, The Furnace*—there are single lyrical numbers, separated arias, for minor characters which expand rather uninteresting roles and add nothing to the action. Ellen Orford's arias are particularly unsatisfactory in this respect—nothing in them illuminates in any degree her relationship with Grimes or shows what he sought from her (or saw in her), unless the point is that as the mother-substitute he craves she is as illusory as the home he identifies her with: too critical and untrustful (of Grimes) and too undiscriminating in her protective care. To a much less disturbing extent, Bianca's aria of Lucretia's girlhood, Florence Pike's aria at the beginning of the fête scene, Cecil's song of government, and the Traveller's opening passage in *Curlew River* are demonstrably aria moments, and indicate that Britten's approach to opera includes and enjoys the separate along with the continuous.

Continuity of form, however, exists virtually throughout the tauter dramas of *Billy Budd* and *The Turn of the Screw*, with large-scale movements in the former and compact vocal

* Opera is continually in search of not so much first principles as pre-historic principles, seeking to justify its art by the conventions of previous ages and literary forms. On the day I am writing this Harrison Birtwistle says of his new work, *Monodrama*: "Our inspiration has been Greek tragedy, which originally evolved from a competition in which one character changed masks and so identity, and that's what happens in our work . . ." (*The Times*, 30 May 1967).

episodes corresponding to the instrumental variations in the latter. The near absence of aria style (single lyrical numbers) in these operas results in the near absence of recitative with the consequence that all the characterisation is more economical and compressed: from all the music the Governess sings, throughout the opera, we could deduce an aria (we have the Soliloquy, "Lost in my labyrinth", but this states rather than develops her mental condition: it has aria style without fully having aria function)—the material is there, a series of variations of what, in my chapter on *The Screw*, I called the Dramatic Theme; but it is incorporated into the scenes, to run parallel to the more expansive instrumental variations. Britten is most often concerned with such monothematic processes; hence the large number of actual passacaglia and variations (in *Lucretia*, *The Screw*, *The Dream*, and *The Furnace*, for example). This approach turns the whole of a very motivically constructed opera—*Lucretia* or *Budd*—into a vast set of variations superimposed on the number-by-number forms, an apt structure in which to represent the singleness of purpose of his operas, the narrow concentration on the drama, the comparative lack of contrasting subsidiary material. The multi-plots of the *Dream* have, predictably, been cut by one in the reduction of the Theseus scenes and what is left is simply three dramas—the faeries, the lovers, the mechanicals—each worked out to a considerable extent in monothematic structures.

Britten's approach to his libretti is less of a constant than his approach to the music because of the great variety of individual personalities he has worked with. Since we have available only the results, not the process, of collaboration, I shall try to infer Britten's approach to the libretti from assessing the extent of their influence on two essentially musical aspects of the operas: characterisation and style.

To say that a libretto is constructed to be expanded is not to deprecate but to define its function. Characterisation, for the librettist, is necessarily an inexact art. Many of his actual words will inevitably be lost to an audience which has not seen the score (nothing of the total sound of the music need be lost in this way), and even hearing the words, could a first-time audience disentangle the sense of Collatinus's aria, "Those who love create fetters which liberate" or even the syntax of the entire chorus beginning "Who holds himself apart lets his pride rise" from *Peter Grimes*? The situations the librettist creates may take on a different emphasis from the time scale of the music over which he has no control. Did, for example, the librettists of *Billy Budd* intend and foresee the exact degree of impetuosity with which Vere sweeps aside Claggart's carefully built-up case against Billy—"Nay, you're mistaken . . ." (a single crotchet rest before Vere's words would make a considerable difference to the impact of his character here) and the incredible and most unoperatic speed with which he acts after Claggart's death? Britten's librettists have a more substantial problem—or degree of abrogation—than many others, since his operas are so often wholly psychological dramas in which the characterisation is more important than the plot, in which we could say that it becomes the plot. And characterisation in this depth is basically developed in the music.

It is a result, then, of the kind of operas Britten writes, that a great many characters exist far more vitally in their music than in their words: Gloriana, Vere, Oberon, the Madwoman, Nebuchadnezzar. Some exist almost wholly in the music: Grimes, Albert Herring, Quint, Flute, and, rather strangely, the Male Chorus in *Lucretia*. These names do not only imply the extent of the intrinsically musical dimensions of these dramas. Eight of the above ten roles were originally created by Peter Pears and it seems quite transparent that the musical personality of this very great singer has had a considerable impact on the operas—at least as much impact as the librettists in the field of characterisation. It is an impact not always for their good. The unmistakable prominence of the Pears role in any of the operas has been the main cause of prevalent misunderstandings about the structure of *Gloriana*, and alters, if it does not destroy, the balance between the two ghosts in *The Turn of the Screw*. It may also account for some of the unsatisfactory elements in *Lucretia*. The fact that Tarquinius appears far less vital in his own music than in that which the Male Chorus sings about him results in the ambiguous motivation of his character: Tarquinius is the one blank face in an otherwise scrupulously characterised drama, and this is, I think, because the expression of his character is spilt between the two roles, and more effective in the narrator than the actor. However, there is much on the credit side— the musical dimensions of Grimes, Quint, and the Madwoman would have been at least a little different if they had been written for another singer. And Albert Herring, inconsistent as he now is, would not have been worth writing an opera about on the basis of the libretto.

To return to the libretti—their influence on the style of the operas is perhaps surprisingly more positive than their contribution to the characterisation. The "gossip" choruses in *Peter Grimes* manage to sound representational in spite of the clumsy words, but how much more spontaneous the trial scene could have been if the music had not been chained to the turgid diction and ponderous sentence lengths of the choruses here—to find how much we have only to compare these with the wholly apt effect of the "Peter Grimes" halloos in the last act, where Britten is free of the unhelpful text. *Lucretia* poses a different problem, for in a chamber opera and without a Chorus it is harder to escape from the text. That *Lucretia* is, until the return of Collatinus in the last scene, more a setting of words than a primarily musical expression of the drama is a result of the conspicuous and rather complex libretto. The chamber-opera medium can project the rich image-packed style of Duncan's libretto with more communication than in a full opera; and the texture of the text has had a discernible influence on the style, and in particular it has necessitated the clarity and precise translation into musical phrases of the recitative.

There is scope, however, for a chamber opera to have a simpler libretto: *The Screw* seems to me to be one of the most intelligent libretti Britten has set. If we compare the characters of the Governess and Quint as they are presented to the composer, we can see this difference: the character of the Governess is fully worked out in the text and the expression of it is sufficiently direct—"I have failed!" . . . "I am useless!" . . . "O Why, Why did I come?"—for the music not merely to set the words but to vivify them unforgettably. And yet the music does not add anything to the character of the Governess which is not indicated in the words. Quint, on the other hand, is handed over to the composer to be a substantially musical character—"Miles!"—his words cannot be too explicit, since they are all extra to the original story; but Quint, as Henry James created him, does not need to speak, simply to be—and this the libretto allows, and the music enables, him to do. His words are allusive and indirect and the music has to have its motive force in his character, not in these words. The closest identification of intention between composer and librettist occurs in the Parables and particularly *Curlew River*. It is the more apparent because this work was a "special case" for both,* and the starting-point was not a one-sided, purely literary source, but a finished performance— a vision of the *impact* of the completed work before either the exact end or the means had been worked out. This unusual circumstance must have contributed to the superb aptness of the libretto for the intense simplicity of the musical style; and the unrepetitiveness of both permits a very compressed and

* *Curlew River* "was generated by the strong response, at quite different times, of the composer and the librettist to performances in Japan of the Medieval *Nō*-plays . . ." (William Plomer, in a programme note to *The Furnace*).

rich dramatic language to emerge. Opera after *Curlew River* is a much less blunt instrument!

In the previous chapters of this book we have seen what immensely individual operas Britten has created. It is, nevertheless, now my aim to show that Britten's choice of drama is as predictable as is his expression of it. The dramas he choses to approach have predictably recurrent themes—themes which deal with aspects of power, evil, suffering, and increasingly specifically Christian solutions. And most conspicuously, themes which produce common characters: the range of characters in Britten's operas is not nearly as great as the range of operas. Thus we have indisputably Grimes's apprentice (or both of them while we are about it) generating Sam in *The Little Sweep* and the Madwoman's son in *Curlew River*. These are the complete innocents. By including corrupted innocence we can add the Novice in *Billy Budd*, Miles in *The Screw*, and possibly, tantalisingly, Lucretia. Peter Grimes is a richer starting-point. The obvious path is the downwards one in degrees of brutality: Tarquinius, the Stranger (in *Curlew River*), Black Bob (in *The Little Sweep*), and Claggart. As a mature, comparative innocent, sacrificed to a community, Grimes could also claim such surprising descendants as Albert Herring, Billy Budd, and the three young men of *The Burning Fiery Furnace*. Vere's problems and behaviour also re-echo through recurring situations in the canon. His closest *alter ego* is Gloriana—both are forced to sacrifice what they love for what they believe to be the good of the people in their charge. So does Nebuchadnezzar, who is let off rather lightly from the burdens of kingship, since he has the Astrologer instead of a conscience, to make the wrong decision for him, and a miracle to relieve him of the consequences. These correspondences indicate some of the repetitive ground of the operas—ground which is repeated only to be additionally illuminated by Britten's successive treatment of it.

The dramas that Britten has chosen are, with only one

exception (the *Dream*), essentially moral ones, though this is not to imply that there is anything facile in the clarity with which he portrays good and evil in conflict: Quint presents a very attractive picture of evil, and Grimes a very unattractive one of innocence. The moral problems are, however, usually unambiguous: for Lucretia, for Vere, for the Governess, and for Nebuchadnezzar the situations they face seem at the time insoluble predicaments, but we, the audience, are never left in any doubt about the total issues involved.

Britten, then, deals almost exclusively with themes of good and evil. He is apparently more interested in the effect than the cause of evil. Black Bob and Quint are the only Devils— the only completely unredeemable personifications of evil—in the canon. Claggart, chiefly because of his very beautiful arias (and given a sense of history in the audience), is human enough to be understandable, and could be played for sympathy, I imagine. The Astrologer probably acted according to his principles—that they were unenlightened and that he was incapable of recognising good when he saw it is no grounds for condemnation in our time. Tarquinius is curiously and unsatisfyingly innocent beside Junius, who acts in his turn with more expediency than malice. The Stranger in *Curlew River* does not even appear in the opera: he is probably more a foreigner, an outlander, like Tarquinius and the Astrologer, than a sadist. The victims of evil, however, are fully drawn, even when they do not sing in the opera— Grimes's apprentices—or appear in human form—the Madwoman's son. Sam and the Novice have a restrained eloquence that is completely moving. For these young victims, evil almost invariably results in physical pain (it is symptomatic of Miles's precocity that it brings him mental torment) and the music is much concerned to portray this. We are far more involved in the Novice's suffering than Billy's because the music conveys the distress of his ordeal more vividly than Billy's. (Does anyone find Billy a fully sympathetic character?)

For the mature sufferer—Gloriana, Vere, Nebuchadnezzar—evil does not appear in the person of a tormentor, but exists in circumstances, and results in the mental pain of crises of judgement. Vere is the only one of these decision-makers to express the actual agony of the crisis—but then he is the only one of them to understand what is at stake: an Abraham-and-Isaac figure. The *Dream* is the only opera outside the moral premise. It enjoys quite amoral principles and standards. It contains no crises of judgement and no physical pain. The only distress is brought about by the inept wielding of an arbitrary power. Probably for these reasons it is a work which delights, but with which we do not remain involved after the final curtain.

The other operas are designed to awake more than a response to the music. They share a personality quite external to the diverse subject-matter of the libretti and scores. The hallmarks of Britten's approach to opera are the attitude of style and the extra-musical themes which are consonant with the character of the series as an unfinished whole and constitute the musical character of the composer.

c.1